GOODBYE TO POPLARHAVEN

Goodbye to Poplarhaven
Recollections of a Utah Boyhood

by

Edward A. Geary

with illustrations by
Ralph H. Reynolds

University of Utah Press
Salt Lake City, Utah
1985

Library of Congress Cataloging-in-Publication Data

Geary, Edward A., 1937–
    Goodbye to Poplarhaven.

    1. Geary, Edward A., 1937–   2. Huntington
(Utah)—Biography.   3. Huntington (Utah)—Social
life and customs.   I. Title.
F834.H77G43   1985   979.2'57   85-7512
ISBN 0-87480-249-0

To my mother and to the memory of my father.

"... *le souvenir d'une certaine image n'est que le regret d'un certain instant; et les maisons, les routes, les avenues, sont fugitives, hélas, comme les années.*"
—*Marcel Proust*, A la recherche du temps perdu

Contents

I

1. Disorder and Early Joy   3
2. The Town on the Prickly Pear Flat   9
3. Water in the Ditch   21
4. Grandpa's Place   31
5. Memorable Conflagrations of My Early Years   39
6. Hying to Kolob   45

II

7. Why I Believe in Santa Claus   59
8. Winter Chores   63
9. The Only Game in Town   67
10. Spring   71
11. Haying   75
12. Three Cheers   85
13. Going Back to School   91
14. The Girls Across the Valley   97
15. The Mill   101
16. Harvest Home   105
17. Roundup   111
18. Politics   115

III

19. The Girl Who Danced with Butch Cassidy   121
20. The Ward Teacher   131
21. A Season on the Mountain   143
22. The Farther Field   153
23. Goodbye to Poplarhaven   159

ACKNOWLEDGMENTS

"Water in the Ditch," "Memorable Conflagrations of My Early Years," "Why I Believe in Santa Claus," "Winter Chores," "The Only Game in Town," "Spring," "Haying," "Three Cheers," "Going Back to School," "The Girls Across the Valley," "The Mill," "Harvest Home," "Roundup," and "Politics" first appeared in a different form and under different titles in the Salt Lake City *Deseret News*. Reprinted with the permission of the *Deseret News*. "Disorder and Early Joy," "Grandpa's Place," "Hying to Kolob," "The Girl Who Danced with Butch Cassidy," and "Goodbye to Poplarhaven" first appeared in a different form in *Dialogue: A Journal of Mormon Thought*. Reprinted with permission of *Dialogue*.

AUTHOR'S NOTE

Those readers who are familiar with southeastern Utah will recognize the town on the Prickly Pear Flat as Huntington. I call it Poplarhaven not to conceal a reality but to reflect my awareness that the place as I experienced and remember it will inevitably be different in some respects from the place that others have known.

EDITOR'S NOTE

Ralph Reynolds was a prominent, award-winning graphic artist and book designer in Utah for many years, working from his own studio, from his agency, and from the offices of the Church of Jesus Christ of Latter-day Saints and Deseret Book Company. These drawings, made during the latter part of his career, are not meant to depict particular places, but, like Geary's Poplarhaven, are an artist's response to the rural experience. Mr. Reynolds died November 15, 1984.

I

Disorder and Early Joy

The *Farm Journal* used to arrive at our house every month bearing on its cover a color photograph of an immaculate Midwestern farmstead or sometimes a scene of autumn in New England. I remember gazing in wonderment at those gleaming white houses and red barns, complete with weather vanes, the painted rail fences enclosing handsome cattle in the pastures, the endless rows of corn, the maple-covered hills. There was nothing remotely like that in our landscape. Nor did we have anything resembling the shiny new tractors and mechanized dairy houses and scientific hog-raising facilities that filled the pages of the magazine. The one feature that struck a familiar note was a monthly cartoon called "Peter Tumbledown." Peter Tumbledown was a ragged old man with a goat-like beard, a corncob pipe, and a long-suffering wife. He was the representative bad example, the blemish on the face of progressive agriculture, the lazy farmer whose place was cluttered with broken-down equipment, hungry dogs, and wandering pigs. He was meant to be an object of ridicule, but I rather liked him and thought it was too bad he didn't live in rural Utah, where he would have been right at home.

Of the dozen or so visual characteristics by which geographers identify the traditional Mormon village, about half are signs of dilapidation or neglect: unused hay derricks; unpainted barns; inside-out granaries whose exposed stud walls give them a forever unfinished look; weed-grown roadsides; "Mormon fences" made of uneven "winny-edge" boards; neglected, overgrown orchards; and dead or dying trees lining the streets. Some of these elements are the relics of time, once-useful things that have fallen into decay. But even in its earliest years, Mormon country was characterized by a certain indifference to neatness. Not that there was anything disorderly about Brigham Young or his design for the settlements. On the contrary, he seemed to envision an earthly paradise. "Cultivate the earth," he preached, "and cultivate your minds. Build cities, adorn your habitations, make gardens, orchards and vineyards, and render the earth so pleasant that when you look upon your labors you may do so with pleasure, and that angels may delight to come and visit your beautiful locations."

That the reality failed to measure up to this vision was a constant source of irritation for Brigham Young. "Were I now to go into one of your houses," he declared on one occasion, "perhaps I should hear the mistress inquiring for a dishcloth; but Sal does not know where it is: the last she saw of it little Abraham or Joe was playing with it outdoors. Where is the milk-pail? Turned bottom-side up on the hog-pen." Fifty years later, Mormon authority J. Golden Kimball complained that "in our beautiful Utah" one might get the impression that "nearly everybody is slipshod; barns, houses, out-buildings are fast going to ruin. The front yards are weed-grown; the fences down and hid by weeds; no flowers, no lawns, no vegetable gardens, no family orchards, or if there is, the trees are old, sickly, and neglected." Down to the present day, Mormon leaders still issue periodic counsel urging church members to tidy up their homes and yards. It is pure Peter Tumbledown.

To grow up in rural Utah is to inherit a tradition of unpainted outbuildings, rickety fences, and superannuated farm implements, a world held together with baling wire. A friend of mine who has lived in other parts of the country has observed that for some mysterious reason a true Utahn cannot be happy unless he has an old Buick rusting away in the back yard.

In my case, it wasn't a Buick but a 1923 Dodge with wood-spoked wheels, decaying gently under an apple tree next to Grandpa's toolshed. (The *new* Dodge was a 1934 model which served until 1949 when the steering wheel came off in Grandma's hands while she was driving downtown.) The side curtains had disappeared long ago, and the chickens sometimes laid eggs in a corner of the back seat where the cotton poked through the brittle fabric, but I thought it was a fine car, with its adjustable windshield and thick steering wheel and the spark-advance lever that you could move back and forth. It was a fine car, but there were even better things in Grandpa's yard, including an old threshing machine with chutes and pulleys and hatches that opened up to reveal wondrous inner workings. Best of all, though, was the steam engine that had once powered the thresher, a monster of a machine with cleated iron wheels, massive boiler, and tall smokestack. When you clambered up to the operator's perch, you discovered such an abundance of levers and gauges that there was nothing left to desire in life—except that you might fire up the boiler once more and set the ponderous vehicle in motion. I dreamed of steaming down a farm lane at three miles an hour, of pulling the whistle cord to send a mournful wail across the fields and hear the answering howl of the neighborhood dogs.

The old Dodge, the threshing machine, and the steam engine were all casualties of the Second World War, gathered up, to my great regret, in the scrap iron drive of 1942–43. But even after these losses, I lived on in a savenger's paradise. There were always interesting things to be found at the town dump up on Rowley Flat. Nobody in our town had heard of sanitary landfill in those days. Whenever you wanted to get rid of something, whether it be bloated cows or drowned kittens, unburnable refuse from the trash barrel or derelict automobile bodies, too far gone even for scrap iron, you simply dumped it on the flat. The dead animals made for some olfactory unpleasantness, but otherwise the dump was a sensory delight, with shards of broken glass glittering like jewels in the sunlight and an inexhaustible variety of shapes: washtubs, bathtubs, cookstoves, wagon wheels, broken baby buggies and tricycles, and a brass bucket discarded for no apparent reason except a small hole in the bottom. There were the sounds of wind whistling across the chimney hole of an old stove and of all the thumps and thunks and plinks that rewarded the throwing of a rock, and a wonderful range of tactile sensations as well, from the gritty texture of rust on an old dishpan to the smoothness of a lump of melted glass dug out of the ashes. Surely Wallace Stegner was right when he observed, of another small-town refuse pile, "The dump was our poetry and our history."

As good as the stuff at the dump was, though, the accumulations that filled people's yards and cellars and sheds were even better. These things had not been discarded, but simply *put* somewhere in the expectation that they might come in handy someday. They represented a world of unrealized possibilities, a reservoir of potential awaiting a creative application. And so, for example, when Grandpa wanted to make me a toy threshing machine (this was after the real one had been hauled away), he had only to step into the toolshed to put his hands on an empty powder box, spools of various sizes to make pulleys, and a bit of copper tubing to fashion into a crank for operating power.

Poplarhaven people saved more things than they ever found uses for, but they did use a lot of the things they saved. One serviceable mowing machine could often be made from two worn-out ones, for example, and two or three old cars or trucks could make one doodlebug. A doodlebug was a homemade tractor built by stripping the body from a car, shortening the frame, putting truck wheels on the rear to improve the traction, and adding a second transmission behind the first to provide lower gearing. Doodlebugs really weren't much good as tractors, but they were unexcelled as off-road vehicles, and there were doodlebug trails up and down all the hills around town.

Some sociologists regard the tendency to save and adapt worn-out things as a symptom of poverty, but I think there is more to it than that. The things that we have used, that show the marks of our use, are signs that we have existed, tangible records of our persistence through time. Clinging to such objects is a way of clinging to life. At any rate, that is how I account for Andrew Anderson's attachment to his old truck.

Andrew Anderson had started out as a peddler, hauling produce to the coal camps, first by team and wagon and later by truck. Over the years he acquired considerable land and cattle, but he continued to operate his truck, taking livestock to market for other farmers. The truck I can remember was surely not his first, but it was the one he had grown old with. Both of them were well worn. The truck was full of dents and rattles, with much baling wire to keep it from falling apart. Andrew Anderson had lost most of his hearing and much of his strength, and he drove his truck much as he had driven his team in earlier days. Horses know where they are going, and you can relax the reins occasionally and let your attention wander without getting into trouble.

As both truck and driver grew less roadworthy, Andrew Anderson's family tried to persuade him to give up driving, but he steadfastly refused. Then, one winter evening when he went out to feed his cattle, he fell into a wash and lay there in the cold for hours before he was discovered. He contracted pneumonia as a result of the exposure, and everybody assumed that if the experience didn't kill him it would surely force him to retire. Grandpa and Grandma went to visit him during his convalescence and found him in a reflective mood. "I guess I'm getting old," he said. "I've got to cut back. I think I'll give up everything but the truck."

I feel that I am growing closer to Andrew Anderson with each passing year. I am growing closer to my grandfather too, and understand better why, though he was a very orderly man, he held onto so many things that most people would regard as junk. Grandpa's toolshed was full of such stuff, old branding irons, bits of harness, half-empty cans of neatsfoot oil, broken teeth from the mowing machine, and odds and ends left over from plumbing and wiring and carpentry projects through the years. Before my time, Grandpa had operated a general store in addition to his farm. When he went out of business, he brought the fixtures home and stored them in the toolshed, the garage, the spare bedrooms. There were sturdy oak cases with sliding doors; a rack with a mirror on it and the words "J & P Coats" embossed in gold; a cabinet containing dozens of tiny drawers in which could be found interesting things of all descriptions: bunches of white tags hanging from loops of string, thin folders of cigarette papers, unused salesbooks with "Geary Mercantile, Where the Dollar Gets Its Value" printed at the top of each page. One case in the toolshed had once held powdered ginger root, and the pungent aroma remained for us to draw in with every breath as we played. Years later, I walked past the open door of a Chinese grocery in San Francisco and caught the unexpected smell of ginger. Like the taste of Proust's Madeleine, that whiff of ginger instantaneously called up a vision of the toolshed. I could feel the earthen floor under my bare feet, and see the slanting beams of light where the sun shone through cracks in the walls and illuminated a column of dust motes, and I could sense all around me the rich store of things, hung on the walls, stuffed in bins, protruding from the dark recesses under the granary floor: so many, many things, and every one of them just the sort of thing that might come in handy someday.

I don't know how Grandpa accumulated it all in a single lifetime. I have amassed a fair amount of clutter myself, but it lacks the character of the things I grew up with. I am coming to realize that the only way to recover that joyous treasure trove is to go back to rural Utah. I'll probably never do it, but I am keeping my eyes open for an old farmstead in a forgotten valley somewhere. I am looking for a central-hall "Nauvoo-style" house and a sway-backed barn that has never known a coat of paint (except perhaps for a faded sign on the side advertising Scowcroft's Never-Rip Overalls). I want an inside-out granary with a set of deer antlers nailed above the door. I want a summer apple tree, and an apricot, and a few hollyhocks growing at random in the dooryard. I am looking for a place whose occupants never threw away anything that might come in handy someday. There will be a broken harrow next to the pigpen, a lopsided grindstone leaning against the coalshed, a rusty dump rake by the cellar, and maybe, just maybe, a steam engine standing in quiet dignity out behind the chicken coop.

TWO

The Town on the Prickly Pear Flat

*You count me out ten, fifty, a hundred, five hundred or a thousand
of the poorest men and women you can find in this community;
with the means that I have in my possession, I will take these ten,
fifty, hundred, five hundred, or a thousand people, and put them
to labor; but only enough to benefit their health and make their
food and sleep sweet unto them, and in ten years I will make that
community wealthy. . . . they shall . . . ride in their carriages,
have fine houses to live in, orchards to go to, flocks and herds and
everything to make them comfortable.*

—*Brigham Young*

That, in a nutshell, was Brigham Young's philosophy of community
building: the faith in the power of work, the fearlessness of risk, the
confidence of success. It was not merely a theoretical program, but
one tested repeatedly over the thirty years that he directed Mormon
colonization in the West. Some colonies failed, and the tumbleweed
blows today across abandoned fields. But most of the four-hundred-
odd towns and villages that Brigham Young planted grew and flourished, at least up to a point. If the inhabitants didn't exactly get rich
in ten years, they did have comfortable homes, orchards, flocks,
herds, and a community that worked.

The Mormon village, the typical unit of settlement, owed something to the New England villages from which Brigham Young and
many other early Mormons had come, and something to Joseph
Smith's "Plat of the City of Zion," a town planned but never built in
western Missouri. The City of Zion was to have been one mile square,
with wide streets and uniform residential lots of one-half acre each to
allow room for orchards and gardens. A space for public buildings was
provided at the center of the townsite, and all barns and stables were
to be outside of town, along with the farmland, so that the residents
could enjoy the benefits of community life while still maintaining an
agrarian economy. As designed, the city had room for about twelve
hundred families and was not to be expanded. Instead, additional

cities of the same design were to be developed to accommodate population growth.

This plan required some modification to fit conditions in Utah. Many of the oases on which settlements were established were too small to provide for as large a population as was envisioned for the City of Zion. Moreover, the arrangement of the residential lots in the City of Zion would have made it difficult to supply them with irrigation water. A typical solution, and the one chosen in Poplarhaven, was to retain the mile-square townsite but make the lots much larger, four lots to a ten-acre block, allowing for a population of about 250 families. The farmland still surrounded the village, but animals were kept in town, with barn, corrals, and cow pasture joining the orchard and garden on the big lots.

Scores of these villages were established in the valleys of Utah and eastern Idaho in the decades after 1847. Most of them were settled by "call," as the church leaders selected settlers and often formed an ecclesiastical organization under a bishop even before they set out for the new location. Those called would include people skilled in the crafts necessary to build and operate a community: surveyors, sawyers, carpenters, blacksmiths, millers, midwives, teachers, musicians. And establishing a new town was not necessarily a once-in-a-lifetime experience. Some people received a new call every few years, becoming in effect professional pioneers.

While the settlers sometimes moved on to other locations, the settlements themselves soon gained a look of permanence as the shade trees matured and brick and stone houses replaced the first log or plank dwellings. Because of the scarcity of irrigation water, the villages usually reached the limits of their arable land and thus of their population within the first few years, and new communities were needed for the next generation and for the stream of immigrants that continued to flow in from Britain and Scandinavia. Most of the suitable locations in the core region had been occupied by the 1870s, and the Mormons began to send out tentacles of settlement into Arizona and southern Colorado, eventually reaching as far as Alberta, Canada, and Chihuahua, Mexico. They also took another look at the less fertile and accessible areas closer to the center. The rugged country of eastern Utah, separated from the rest of the territory by a chain of mountains and high plateaus, had largely been ignored in earlier years (one exploring party had returned with the report that the country was good for nothing but "to hold the earth together"), and by the mid-1870s it was one of the last frontiers in the contiguous United States.

West of the Wasatch Plateau, in central Utah, lay the Sanpete Valley, teeming with young families in need of land. Directly to the east, only twenty-five miles away as the crow flies (though fifty miles by wagon in the summer and more than 100 in the winter), was an area of one thousand square miles known as Castle Valley. The soil did not appear to be very good, but there was plenty of it, and several year-round creeks flowed from the plateau. On 22 August 1877, after some preliminary surveys, Brigham Young issued a formal call for settlers to go to Castle Valley, "as we are anxious to see a good, strong settlement of Latter-day Saints established. . . ." He went on to advise the church leaders in Sanpete to "choose good, energetic, God fearing young men, whether single or with families, and others who can be spared without interfering with the interests of the settlements in which they now reside, such ones as will be a strength to the new settlement, and an aid to its growth in all that we, as Latter-day Saints, desire to see increase upon the earth." It was the last settlement call issued by Brigham Young. One week later, on 29 August, the Great Colonizer was dead at the age of seventy-six. There used to be a saying in Poplarhaven that as soon as Brother Brigham called people to Castle Valley the Lord took him. This was said in such a way as to leave it uncertain whether he was taken because his mission had now been completed or because he had finally gone too far.

Few places on the earth could have looked less promising for settlement than Castle Valley in 1877. Except for the cottonwoods along the creeks, the valley was treeless from the steep escarpment of the plateau to the distant buttes of the San Rafael Swell. The mancos shale soil ("blue clay," it is called locally) supported a thin growth of shadscale and prickly pear, the sparse vegetation that could survive on seven inches of rainfall. The Indians called it "Blow Valley" because of the continual dry winds, and they avoided the place, claiming that the water made their women's necks grow large. (Goiter trouble afflicted the settlers as well. I can remember several older women who had the characteristic swellings on their necks, and my Great-grandmother Wakefield died of the condition.) Before the Rio Grande Western Railroad was built through the northern part of the valley in 1883, traveling to the nearest outside towns required a three-day wagon trip in the summer and five or six days in the winter, if the road was passable. The isolation and the primitive living conditions must have been especially difficult for the women, who came from communities where life had begun to be more comfortable. Legend has it that when Hannah Seeley (whose husband, Orange Seeley, had been chosen to lead the settlement on Cottonwood Creek, ten miles south of Poplarhaven) first caught sight of the valley she exclaimed, "Damn the man who would bring a woman to a place like this!" Another young wife, Mary Ann Brown, who had grown up in an English home of some refinement, was brought by her husband to a dugout by the creek only to discover that a neighbor had locked his pigs inside. She cried, "Oh, Charlie, I've lived in many a place, but I never thought I'd have to live with the pigs!"

Despite the difficulties, however, the settlements grew rapidly, and within four or five years most of the names that have come down through the generations in Poplarhaven were already there. From Sanpete Valley came the Coxes, Joneses, Guymons, Ottesons, Collards, Shermans, and Johnsons, among others. The Leonards and Gordons came from Rush Valley in western Utah, Brashers and Howards from the Bear Lake country, Gardners from Grouse Creek. From Utah Valley there were the Granges, from Heber Valley Neilsons and Andersons, from Pahvant Valley the McKees. The Marshalls, Robbinses, and Allens came from the Virgin River settlements, and the Rowleys and McElprangs from the San Juan Mission at Bluff.

In the older Utah settlements, the people had simply squatted on the land and sought to gain legal ownership later. But Castle Valley was settled under the homestead laws, which required the settlers to live on their farms for several years in order to obtain title. In most regions the homestead system produced a scattered rural population, but not in Castle Valley. People built temporary dugouts or cabins on their homesteads, but with the vision of the City of Zion before them they laid out a mile-square townsite on the Prickly Pear Flat, a tableland above the creek, and erected a log meetinghouse at its center even before they began work on the canal that would water the town. As they proved up on their homesteads, most families moved into town, erecting dwellings in a sequence that can still be traced through surviving structures: log or plank cabins at first, then central-hall houses of lumber and adobe, and finally, after William Green established his brickyard in the 1890s, larger houses of a beautiful buff-toned brick. The houses were set on the corners of the blocks, with the farm buildings in the block interiors. Thus each family had three "front-door" neighbors in the other houses that faced the same intersection, and three "back-door" neighbors in the other occupants of the same block. As in other Mormon settlements, the people felt an urgency to plant trees in the treeless landscape. Even before the town ditch was completed, many families had planted saplings on their lots, keeping them alive by hauling water from the creek in barrels. Soon there were fast-growing willows and box elders to shade the dooryards and more stately locusts, ashes, black walnuts, and catalpas. A Mr. Sweet came to town as an agent for Stark Brothers Nurseries, and most people planted a few fruit trees to allay a hunger that could not be satisfied with bullberry pudding and chokecherry jam. (When the nurseryman knocked at the door of Leander Lemmon, a rancher who had been the first settler on the creek, he introduced himself by saying, "My name is Sweet." "My name is sour," Lemmon replied.) A short-lived silkworm experiment led to the planting of dozens of mulberry trees whose bland fruit stained hands and faces and sidewalks down to my own time. As a windbreak, the settlers lined the streets with rows of lombardy poplars whose straight, erect lines emphasized the geometrical regularity of the town, its foursquare presence in the vast space of the valley, as if to say to the formless wilderness, "We are here, and we mean to stay."

My Great-grandfather Wakefield was one of those who answered Brigham Young's call, coming over the mountain from Sanpete in 1878, the second year of the settlement. Johnny Wakefield was a small man with only one eye, the other having been gouged out by the ragged horn of a milk cow when he was a boy. He died before I was born, but I grew up on my grandmother's reverent stories and the anecdotes told at the family reunions that were held each summer on Grandpa's shady lawn. When Johnny Wakefield arrived in the valley, he found the riverbottom land all claimed, so he staked out 160 acres on the flat. He did not intend to farm the entire homestead himself. His brother Thomas and brothers-in-law Milas and Joseph Johnson were also moving to Castle Valley, and the plan was to divide the acreage four ways. Many of the early settlers were related to one another, and it was a common practice to divide a homestead in this way. Few families farmed more than forty acres at first, and some farms were as small as ten or fifteen acres.

After marking his claim, Johnny Wakefield returned to Fountain Green to earn money for the move by working at a sawmill. He came back to Castle Valley the next fall, crossing the mountain with a sizeable party of settlers. They camped overnight in Scad Valley, on top of the plateau, and Johnny overheard some of the other men planning to claim the very piece of land he had marked out for himself. He left his team and wagon in the care of Uncle Jody Johnson and hiked through the night to reach the valley, coming down the Left Hand Fork of the creek, where there was no road. Early the next morning, a Sunday, he reached Elias Cox's sawmill in Mill Fork, and Bishop Cox offered him a ride on into town. While he waited for the bishop to harness the team, Johnny scratched his name and the date, 23 November 1879, on a large rock with a nail that he had in his pocket. We never went up the canyon, when I was a boy, without stopping at that rock to look at the scratchings and hear once more the story of how Johnny Wakefield saved his homestead.

It didn't occur to me then, but the homestead might not have been much worth the saving. It was flat land, easy to till, and close to town, but before he could farm it he had to dig a two-mile-long ditch to bring water from the creek. In later years, when the higher parts of the flat were brought under irrigation, Great-grandpa Wakefield's land turned swampy and unproductive.

While he was working on the Wakefield Ditch, running a small stream of water as he went along to soften the ground for digging, he also put up a one-room log cabin on his homestead, and in the fall of 1880 he brought his wife and children over from Fountain Green. Uncle Fleming, who was eight years old, and Uncle Mide, who was six, remembered walking over the mountain while their mother and their sister Ellis and baby brother Don rode in the wagon with the household goods. Uncle Miley and Uncle Jody Johnson moved their families at the same time, and the three families lived together in the single sixteen-by-eighteen-foot room until February, when the Johnson cabins were finished, the first dwellings built on the townsite.

That was early in 1881. By the fall of 1883, when my Great-grandfather Geary arrived, there were some fifty houses on the Prickly Pear Flat. Poplarhaven had become a town.

My four great-grandfathers stand in my mind as representatives of the kind of men who built the Mormon village and gave it its distinctive character. Johnny Wakefield was the saint, a man whose every act, almost, was governed by faith. He was born in Iowa, shortly after the Mormons were driven from Illinois, and walked across the plains with his widowed mother, in the approved pioneer style. His wife, Julia Johnson, was also born on the frontier, and like her husband she never for an instant wavered in her devotion to her faith and all of its principles and rules. (They met at a party in Fountain Green, where she charmed him with her rendition of "Touch Not the Wine-cup," a song that was sung again at every family reunion. She was fourteen years old at the time. They married a year later.) After he had proved up on his homestead, Johnny Wakefield hooked several teams of horses to his cabin and dragged it up the road to his town lot, where he added several lumber and adobe rooms and set about rearing a large family on a small income. Uncle Perry, the last born, was twenty-eight years younger than Uncle Fleming, but despite the wide range in ages the children were exceptionally close. No family has ever cherished their childhood more deeply; no home can ever have been a more lasting symbol of warmth and love and security.

Johnny Wakefield was a man devoid of worldly ambition, ready to share his last sack of flour (or the single room in his cabin) with anyone who had less. He dreamed dreams and had visions, and could talk reassuringly about those on "the other side." Perhaps in recognition of this comfortable commerce with the hereafter, he was for many years the sexton of the town cemetery and dug hundreds of holes for the deposit of mortal husks while keeping his single eye firmly fixed on the immortal part. He was utterly fearless of natural phenomena and liked nothing better than to sit on the porch and watch a good lightning storm. If a bolt struck nearby, he would say, "By jollies, that was a good one!"—the closest he ever came to profanity. Except for the rock on which he scratched his name, he left no material monuments, but his children revered him to their dying days, and he was, in the opinion of my grandfather (who was an unbiased judge on such matters), the most respected man in town, though he never held important office either civil or ecclesiastical.

If Great-grandpa Wakefield was a saint, Great-grandpa Geary was a builder. His parents were converted to the LDS Church in a dreary factory town in Derbyshire and immigrated to Utah when he was a young child, settling in Round Valley, near Morgan. He grew to manhood there, married Alice Criddle, built a rock house for his young family, and farmed in the summer and worked for the Union Pacific Railroad in the winter. He bore, as my grandfather did and as I do, the old family name of Edward, and he was a man of unusual physical strength and endurance. He was not a pious or saintly man, though he lived respectably and contributed of his time and means to church and community. Nor did he have much personal charm. He was taciturn and moody and could, when he grew irritated, go for the better part of a week without speaking a word to anyone. But he was a man who could see what needed to be done, and do it, an ambitious man, constantly driving himself and others. Among other things he was an expert teamster, so skilled with the bullwhip that he could flick off a chicken's head with it as neatly as with an axe.

When the church issued a call for settlers to go to the Little Colorado River in Arizona, Ed Geary sold his place at Round Valley, packed his belongings into two big trail wagons, and set out with his strong horses and his rather frail wife for the settlement of Saint Johns. He worked on the canal there through the summer of 1883, but by fall he had become convinced that there would rarely be enough water to fill it. Some Mormons looked upon a settlement call as a binding mission, at which they must remain until they were "released," either by another call or by death. But Ed Geary was not a man to subordinate his judgment to anyone else's, so he packed his possessions into the wagons again and returned to Utah, stopping at Poplarhaven. He arrived dead broke, with no place to live, three children under the age of five, and a sick and discouraged wife. Over the next ten years, he had two more children, lost his wife to childbirth complications, sent his two infant daughters to be reared by relatives, lost one son in a typhoid epidemic and another to diphtheria, married again and lost a second wife, then remained for several years in a bachelor's existence with my grandfather, a frail, asthmatic child. Yet in the same period he built canals, hauled timber, transported freight on government contract, invested in machinery, and accumulated land and cattle until he was the biggest taxpayer in the community. He brought the first threshing machine to Poplarhaven, the first steam engine, the first hay fork, the first barbed wire, the first piped water. When he built a new house in the early 1890s, it was a spacious brick structure with floors and finish trim of Oregon pine—the finest house in town.

Although my maternal great-grandparents never lived in Poplar-haven, they were associated with Castle Valley, and they represent additional strains of pioneer stock. Henning Olsen Ungerman was born in Denmark in 1830, joined the LDS Church in 1857, and came to Utah in 1861. He left Denmark with his pregnant wife, Sidsel, and two children. Two-year-old Maria died and was buried at sea. Marie Josephine Atlantic was born and died in the Gulf of Mexico but was buried after they landed at New Orleans. Sidsel made it as far as Florence, Nebraska, before she died, and Henning crossed the plains with only my grandfather, six-year-old Ole Louis, as the remnant of his family. After a year in Utah, he married Christina Mortensen, a young woman who had crossed the plains in the same company, and settled in Spring City, Sanpete County, where he married two plural wives.

Henning Olsen was a saintly man, like Johnny Wakefield, and a builder, like Ed Geary—quite literally a builder as he had been trained as a brickmason in Denmark—but for me he represents the central figure in Mormon community life, the bishop. He was called to Castle Valley in 1881 and settled in Castle Dale, where he served as bishop for fifteen years and had a hand in constructing almost every substantial house or public building that was erected before 1900. He had dropped the Ungerman name for fear that he might be compelled to return to Denmark for military service. There were so many Olsens that the name provided anonymity. As a polygamist, he was father to nineteen children and stepfather to twelve others, though his plural wives were both older than himself. My mother has a woman's aversion to polygamy, but she has always said that at least Grandpa Olsen practiced it in the right spirit, as a way of providing for the widow and the orphan. It cannot be said that his domestic arrangements were entirely harmonious, however. The wives apparently got along well enough, but one of his stepsons became a deputy U.S. marshall and made several attempts to arrest his stepfather. Bishop Olsen spent many hours hiding in the willows by the creek to avoid capture.

The bishop, the builder, the saint were all important contributors to the development of the Mormon village. My fourth great-grandfather represents a different strain, the rancher. Valentine Louis Acord, who was always called by the nickname "Felt," was born in frontier Indiana of Pennsylvania Dutch stock. Orphaned at an early age, he ran away from his guardians and lived for several years with the Sioux Indians. As a young man he married Sarah Georgina Frost, in Iowa, and came west with her family and with his brother Abram, who had married Sarah's sister. The Acord brothers thought they were going to California, but their father-in-law had secretly joined the Mormon Church and intended to stop in Utah. Eventually Sarah and Abram and his wife also became Mormons, and Felt himself was baptized, but he was never more than nominally associated with the church.

Felt Acord got his start as a freighter, hauling manufactured goods from Missouri to Utah, produce from Utah to the Montana mines, and concentrated ore from the mines back to the railhead in the Midwest. It was a profitable operation, and by the time the railroads put him out of business he had made enough money to buy a large herd of cattle. Abram had accumulated some money by working in the Nevada mines, and the two brothers settled in Spring City, where Abram remained, becoming a pillar of the community. But Felt was not one to settle down. After Sarah died, he left my grandmother, who was only two years old, to be reared by another family in Spring City. Though he remarried, he never remained in one spot for very long but took to following his cattle from place to place, always in search of better range. He ranched throughout western Utah and into Arizona, and when the Oklahoma Territory was opened for settlement he moved there. It was there that his youngest son, Art, grew up with a rope in his hand. Art Acord was later to achieve fame as a rodeo performer with the Buffalo Bill Wild West Show and as a cowboy star in silent films.

Felt Acord returned to Utah in his last years, living in Castle Dale near some of his children. He was still a fine figure of a man in his old age and reputedly one of the best judges of horses that the country had ever seen. My mother remembers him walking up to their home at dawn each day from his lodgings in town. He would hammer on the door with his walking stick and call out imperiously, "Daughter! Daughter! Get up and make me some coffee"—a demand that used to irritate my grandmother.

These, then, were some of the founders of the world I inherited. Of course there were many others as well: orators and politicians such as Uncle Miley and Uncle Jody Johnson, one an avid Democrat, the other an equally avid Republican, who ran against each other for the state legislature; teachers such as Uncle Don Woodward, who provided an educational foundation to two generations, and Professor Hardee, the Welsh choirmaster who formed the youth of a frontier town into a polished chorus; women such as "Aunt Jane" Woodward, the closest thing to a doctor in the early community, and Mary Ann Brown, whose memoirs provide the most vivid picture of pioneer life.

This seemed an abundant heritage to me as I was growing up in Poplarhaven, and the town itself seemed abundant: abundant space in the wide streets and the big, shady yards; abundant hay and grain and fruit, stored up in dim cool cellars and gray barns and inside-out granaries; abundant room in the big brick houses, inhabited mostly by old people whose children had grown and moved away, and room too in the old meetinghouse, room enough for everybody in town. This is the Poplarhaven I remember, the rows of poplars running straight beside the irrigation ditches, the meetinghouse steeple, visible from anyplace in town, with the bell that rang each Sunday morning half an hour before meeting time, sending its clear tones over the town on the Prickly Pear Flat, over the clustering mantle of fields, over the barren flats to the walls of the plateau that stood, steep and imposing, like a guardian barrier protecting a way of life.

SWIFT CREEK CAMP
JULY 77
R Reynolds 77

THREE

Water in the Ditch

For the rock and for the river,
The valley's fertile sod
For the strength of the hills we bless thee,
Our God, our fathers' God.
        (Old Mormon hymn, adapted from Felicia Hemans,
        "Hymn of the Vaudois Mountaineers")

The tableland runs down the center of Utah like a massive spinal column a hundred miles long, twenty-five wide, and ten thousand feet high. On maps it is called the Wasatch Plateau. Over in Sanpete Valley, on the west side, they call it Manti Mountain, and that is the name of the national forest that covers much of the high country. In Castle Valley we rarely used either of those names but spoke simply of The Mountains, as though there were no others. We reserved names for individual promontories or segments of the mass: Gentry, East Mountain, Ferron Mountain, The Horn.

A thousand feet of elevation is roughly equivalent to three hundred miles of north latitude, so going up into the mountains is like traveling north to Canada. The change in climate and scenery is what you might expect from a journey of fifteen hundred miles instead of fifteen. The top of the plateau is a broad expanse of valleys and ridges, with spring-fed meadows, shimmering groves of quaking aspen, dense forests of fir on the northern slopes, and open, sage-grey southern slopes brightened throughout the summer by a succession of wildflowers. Snowbanks persist in sheltered coves through August, and stunted trees straggle along the topmost ridges amid wild gooseberry thickets.

To believe the lush beauty of the mountains, however, you must go up into them. From the valley the escarpment looms dry and forbidding, rising stratum upon stratum of cliff and talus slope to where a few pines are silhouetted against the sky like an irregular file of infantry. As seen from the valley, the mountains are not green but rather grey-blue with red patches where the rock appears sunburned. The green flows with the creek out of the canyon, widens to encompass a few thousand acres of farmland surrounding the town, then tapers off and disappears into seventy miles of desert gorges and mesas that stretch eastward to the canyonlands of the Colorado River.

Without the high plateau there would be no Poplarhaven. The moisture captured from the westerly winds by the mountains is vital to all of the checkerboard towns that lie wrapped in their patchwork quilts of farmland throughout Utah. The story of the Mormon village is the story of the water, as the Utah writer Virginia Sorenson has pointed out. It was the necessity of irrigation that largely determined the shape and look of Mormon country. The task of digging and maintaining the irrigation canals was too great for a single family, thus dictating a communal pattern of settlement instead of the individualistic pattern that characterized the fertile Midwest. On the other hand, there was no capital available in the early days to construct massive reclamation works such as have been built in the West in this century. Each community was on its own in supplying labor and machinery, so the systems were relatively small and simple.

You see these irrigation systems everywhere in Mormon country, some of them little changed in a hundred years. The first settlers, anxious to get some land under cultivation, diverted small streams onto the floodplains. Later, more extensive diversion works and longer canals brought water to the higher land. When the highline canals were completed, the lower ditches were sometimes abandoned but sometimes not. As a result, the Mormon landscape is marked by parallel canals, each with its own thicket of trees and shrubs resembling the hedgerows of Europe.

The vital importance of this hydrologic system was impressed upon me from earliest childhood. The snowbanks on the mountains that we could slide down in July were the source, the starting point. The trickling water that saturated the ground at their base fed the springs that gushed, chill and sweet, out of limestone hillsides farther down. The impounded water of the reservoirs did more than mirror the cloudless sky. It was the means of equalizing the seasonal flows, catching some of the spring runoff and saving it for the thirsty crops of midsummer. The long canyon that cut diagonally into the plateau and channeled the runoff from a hundred square miles down to the valley was our veritable lifeline as well as our park and our natural air-conditioning system, pouring out a flood of cool mountain air each evening when the sun went down.

Having grown up in a dry land, I have a fondness for water in all its forms, for the lake, the sea, the rushing mountain stream, the mighty river. But best of all I love the irrigation canal, running quietly between its willow-grown banks, dividing green land from grey, gradually losing its mountain chill as it winds across the valley. No music is sweeter than the soft gurgle of water in the ditch, punctuated by a ripple where the stream runs over a snag or by the plop of a muskrat as it slips from the bank.

The Big Canal ran half a mile above our place. It was not really very big, two or three feet deep and perhaps ten wide, but it was the mother of all the smaller ditches, including the Town Ditch that ran through our front yard. Where the Town Ditch was diverted from the Big Canal, the ditchbank thicket was unusually wide, forming a grove of cottonwoods and willows, a perfect place for secret hideouts. Owls and sparrowhawks nested in hollows in the big trees, and every clump of willows held the bulky form of a magpie nest. Hidden paths led to the water's edge, to pools that only we knew, where we could go skinny-dipping without fear of discovery. Or we could float for miles on old innertubes, drifting lazily through an endless arbor.

The canal was our unofficial swimming pool and marina—unofficial because the people in the downstream hamlet of Lawrence drew their drinking water from it and swimming was officially prohibited—but most importantly it was the main artery of the community's circulation system. In town, a family had to plan its activities around the weekly "water turn." Every spring, each family on a sub-ditch would receive a schedule of water turns, the period of time (depending on the amount of stock they held in the irrigation company) when they could use the stream. Some turns came during daylight hours, when it was easy to irrigate, but some would be at two or three o'clock in the morning. Every minute of a water turn was precious, so no matter when it came the householder would be at the headgate with his flashlight and shovel and gum boots. When the water turn came during the day, the whole family got involved, some coaxing streamlets through the furrows in the vegetable gardens, others carrying bucketfuls to shrubs beyond reach of the ditch, and the younger children splashing barefoot on the flooded lawn.

In the fields the streams ran continuously throughout the irrigation season, and tending water was the first chore in the morning and the last at night. Each field was marked out in plots by its ditches: the cut through the shale hill, the levee across the swale, the cross-ditch that picked up the runoff from the alfalfa and carried it down to the pasture. Every division, every run was known by heart, known like the good shovel whose handle was worn to the shape of the hand and whose spoon bore the marks of dozens of filings and thousands of sods.

This irrigation system, on which the entire welfare of the community depends, has produced its own laws and customs, its officials, heroes, and villains, and a wealth of lore. Every town has a watermaster, whose job it is to apportion the water equitably. Disputes over water rights are common. In the early days they were resolved in bishops' courts, in later times in the civil courts. Sometimes the disputes have led to violence and the criminal courts. Most Utah communities have a memory of some incident in which mayhem was committed with a shovel over a headgate.

Where water is wealth, water cheating is a constant threat. Everybody knows the farmer whose headgate persistently opens up between inspections by the watermaster, or the townsman whose lawn and garden remain a flourishing green while his neighbors' are parched with drought, leading to the suspicion that he is doing a little midnight irrigating at somebody else's expense. I have had my own run-in with irrigation law. One day some friends and I decided to improve our swimming hole by removing some of the planks that regulated the flow of water from the Big Canal to the Town Ditch. Phineas Cook saw us as he rode by on his wagon and reported us to the watermaster. George Gardner was watermaster then, a kindly man, but he remains in my memory a figure of awesome wrath. We never tampered with the boards again.

The first real sign of spring in Poplarhaven, more dependable than the dandelions that bloomed against the south wall of Maurice Jensen's store, was the annual ditch cleaning. No matter how raw or blustery the weather, every man and boy capable of wielding a shovel turned out on an appointed weekend in March to clear the ditches for the upcoming irrigation season. Crews moved up and down the streets in town, cutting back the encroaching grass in the roadside ditches and leaving the sides neatly scalloped. Other crews worked on the canals, hacking at willows, pulling out snags, repairing headgates.

For those of us whose summer work was on the family farm, ditch cleaning was often our first experience at a "real job," where we worked for wages under supervision of someone outside the family. I can remember the spring when I was put on a canal crew under the direction of Jim Wilson, a tough old farmer from Lawrence. In addition to what I learned about physical labor that weekend, I learned that teachers and parents were wrong when they said that swearing was a sign of an impoverished vocabulary. Jim Wilson had plenty of vocabulary, and a good portion of it was cuss words, which he manipulated with a genuine artistry such as I have not encountered before or since. It wasn't that I didn't already know the words he used, but he had a knack for arranging them in fresh combinations and could by a certain inflection give a new turn of meaning to an old expletive. Shakespeare and Joyce would have known how to appreciate Jim Wilson.

Ditch cleaning days were long and sometimes strenuous, but we were glad for a chance to earn some hard cash. Hard cash is not quite the right word, though, as we were paid for our labors at seventy-five cents per hour in water company scrip, redeemable against water assessments the following November. Few of us were willing to wait eight months for our money, so we took our scrip to Clare Guymon's store, where he would redeem it on the spot for eighty cents on the dollar. We accepted the money willingly enough, but we left the store grumbling about old "Pinch," as we called him, and his supposedly grasping ways, which were probably no more than necessary for economic survival in a town where many people were quick to buy on credit but slow to pay their bills.

"Do you know how the Grand Canyon was formed?" someone would ask. "Pinch Guymon lost a dime down a gopher hole."

Then we would go on to other stories, such as the one about the sloppy woman from the North Fields who brought her nursing baby with her one day when she went shopping. Guymon's was not a self-service store. If you wanted to buy something, you stood in front of the counter and pointed it out, and Clare Guymon or one of his clerks would reach it down from the shelf. The woman nursed her baby while she looked at fabric for a dress. Clare Guymon got down bolt after bolt of cloth and laid it out on the counter, while at the same time doing his best to ignore his customer's state of dishabille. Eventually the baby had had enough and began to play at the breast.

"You eat your dinner," the mother scolded, "or else Mr. Guymon will get it!"

A *good* year in southern Utah is one in which the irrigation water lasts through July, and the bad years, the dry years, are much more frequent than the wet ones. Even culinary water was often in short supply when I was a boy. The Bear Canyon spring that was piped down to the town supplied the most delicious water I have ever tasted but not enough of it when people began to sprinkle their lawns to supplement the weekly water turn. Living at the top of the town, we were among the first to run out of water when the storage tanks were drained. We would get a telephone call from Mrs. Sandberg, who was still higher on the line, saying, "The water is going off." Then someone would run to turn off the hose while others began to fill the bathtub and whatever pots and pans were available. Somebody would telephone the people down the street: "The water is going off." We watched the thin streams coming from the taps grow thinner and fail, and heard the sucking sound as air was drawn into the pipes. The water might go off twice or three times a week. Sometimes it came back on after a few hours. Sometimes it took a day or two, for those on the upper end of the line. Until the water returned, we had to get along on whatever supply we had managed to store. Fortunately, we had the ditch out front, and almost every family still had an outhouse in the back yard, having a well-founded distrust of any modern appliance which required a dependable supply of water for its operation.

These were problems we had in normal years. In drought years things were much worse. I remember the drought of the mid-1950s, when we lost the second crop of hay. The great drought of the 1930s was before my time, but I can remember the stories people told about it. In 1934, they say, many normally dependable creeks in southern Utah stopped flowing altogether. In our valley the water got so low that they divided up the Big Canal, letting people at the upper end use the water one week and those on the lower half the next. But it got so bad that the water didn't even reach the end of the canal before the week was up. Finally, they gave up on the crops in the fields and turned the entire stream into the Town Ditch to try to keep the vegetable gardens alive. It got so bad, they say, that you couldn't afford to sweat. It got so bad that you could go up the canyon and see trout sitting on the banks of the creek, waiting for their turn to swim. It got so bad, finally, that Grandpa decided he might as well take a vacation, there being no water to tend. He and Grandma and Frank and Kate Robbins got into the new Dodge and went to California to see the ocean. When they got to the beach the tide was out, and Frank Robbins gazed in alarm at the wide expanse of sand.

"Looky there, Ed," he said. "She's drying up!"

Not everyone shares my fondness for open irrigation canals. They unquestionably represent a danger to young children, and they are not the most efficient means of delivering water. Increasingly now, ditches are giving way to pressurized irrigation systems, especially in populous areas. And even in Poplarhaven, though the Big Canal continues to flow, the Town Ditch is gone, having run its last stream in 1982, exactly one hundred years from the time the water was first turned into it.

No century-old institution should be allowed to pass into oblivion without a modest eulogy, and I doubt if anyone knew the old ditch better than I did. The pioneers made the Town Ditch, but the Town Ditch really made the town, transforming the barren Prickly Pear Flat into a place where things could grow and people could live. For many years the Town Ditch provided the culinary supply as well as the irrigation water. Water for household use was diverted into a cistern connected to a pump in the kitchen, or, more often, simply dipped from the ditch in buckets. A little alum sprinkled on the water helped to settle the mud but did little to inhibit the germs that spread periodic epidemics of typhoid through the town. For Saturday baths or Monday laundry, the ditch water was heated on the kitchen stove in copper boilers.

This system was not entirely satisfactory, especially in the winter when ice made it difficult to keep water running in the ditch, or during spring snow melt when the water might be roily for several weeks. In the summer there was the problem of contamination from the livestock grazing on the watershed. Poplarhaven farmers were mostly cattlemen. Therefore, they didn't see much harm from the cattle on the mountain. But the sheep herds from Sanpete County that grazed on the highest slopes of the plateau were another matter. At the turn of the century, William Howard complained in a letter to the editor that "science has said that running water purifies itself in running seven miles, but during the spring high water and summer rains, the filth from sheep camps comes down from a distance of 25 to 30 miles, and when we dip a bucket of water from our town ditches to drink or cook our food in, and find sheep droppings in it, as we often do, all the science on earth cannot make us believe that it is pure water."

All of that was long before my time. From my earliest memories we had clear water piped in from the Bear Canyon spring. But I knew many people who saw nothing wrong with drinking from the ditch. Old Marion Cox, whose place adjoined one of Grandpa's fields, used to hang empty tin cans on fence posts all along the ditch so that he could dip up a drink whenever he felt like it. I have drunk from the ditch myself on many occasions with no bad effects, only a little anxiety lest I should swallow a water strider.

The most exciting part of the Town Ditch was its beginning, the swift-running weir where it was divided off from the Big Canal, and where I got into trouble with the watermaster. There the water ran so fast that it could sweep you off your feet if you were not careful, and our parents tried, without success, to keep us from playing there. From the weir the ditch flowed uneventfully past the Cook place then dropped down a small hill in two waterfalls. Below the upper fall, which had a drop of only five or six feet, the stream divided into several channels, forming tiny islands in the thicket of willows for fifty yards or so before dropping over the lower fall, which was perhaps ten feet high. This was one of my favorite places, a private wilderness where we could play out whatever fantasy had been stimulated by the latest picture show, whether knights in armor, or pirates, or Ali Baba and the Forty Thieves, or a Zane Grey western. In one movie there was a treasure-filled cave whose entrance was concealed by a waterfall, and I used to imagine that there might be such a place hidden behind our falls, a subterranean chamber lit by torches that illuminated heaps of gold and jewels. When the water was turned out of the canal in the fall, I went to the thicket and probed the shallow hollows formed by the falling water, but I couldn't find the entrance.

From the lower fall, the canal ran to the mill through a gorge that seemed very deep to us. The mill had originally been run by waterpower, and the old conduit that had supplied the waterwheel still spanned the gorge, where it served us as a rather scary footbridge. Below the mill, the canal ran through another thicket of willows, scrub birches, and cottonwoods, with a single volunteer apple tree whose tiny, wormy fruit we devoured eagerly because it was a secret tree. Here we used to race toy boats in the stream or dig roads for our toy cars in the clay banks and build cities of mud. Our house lay midway along this stretch of the canal. My father had grown up beside the Town Ditch and my mother by a similar canal over in Castle Dale, and they included the canal in their landscaping, clearing out the brush and willows and making the lawn slope down to the stream. At the top of the lot they built a small waterfall (too small to have a secret cave behind it), whose music filled all the summers of my childhood.

From our place the canal flowed past Grandpa's orchard then turned at the corner of his lot to run south along the top of town. There was a fine stretch of rapids at the corner, but thereafter the stream flowed quietly, shrinking block by block as successive ditches were diverted off to run along each street and water the town lots. Just past Grandpa's bridge, there was a row of tall cottonwoods, and my cousins hung a rope swing on a high limb of one tree. You grasped the rope as high as you could reach, took a run, and launched out from the ditchbank, soaring over the water and into the lower branches of the tree, then back in a return arc to the landing spot. If you lost your grip, as I did a time or two, the canal would catch you.

Somebody downstream had a family of ducks that used to paddle up the canal as far as Grandpa's place, the mother resembling a quacking tugboat towing a string of fluffy yellow barges, perfectly at home wherever the canal ran. I felt much the same way myself, felt that I could follow the Town Ditch up to its source or down to where the last rill disappeared in a garden furrow without ever leaving home territory. The stream runs underground now, in a pipe, invisible and inaudible. But it also runs deep beneath the surface of memory, where it still gurgles gently between grassy banks, watering the roots and providing sweet refreshment in the dry seasons.

FOUR

Grandpa's Place

The oldest hath borne most: we that are young
Shall never see so much, nor live so long.
                                        —*Shakespeare*, King Lear

When I was very small my grandfather used to take me on his knees
and sing a nursery rhyme in his tuneless way:

> Pace goes the lady
> Pace goes the lady
> Trot goes the gentleman
> Trot goes the gentleman
> Gallop goes the farmer
> Gallop goes the farmer.

With each couplet he bounced his knees higher and faster until as the
farmer I was charging along at a great rate, holding onto Grandpa's
arms for dear life. I have since learned that in the original version of
the rhyme it is the gentleman who gallops while the farmer proceeds
at a hobble-trot on his old plowhorse. Grandpa must have modified
the verse to fit his own sense of the relative dignity of the two stations,
and I certainly would never have questioned the appropriateness of
his version. Who would want to be a mere gentleman if he could be a
farmer?

Grandpa was a farmer, "farmer and stockman," as he put it to
indicate that he ran a hundred head of cattle on the range in addition
to cultivating eighty acres or so. Grandpa himself rarely galloped, in
my day, though he claimed to have had the fastest sleighing team in
town when he was a young man. He usually left Old Nick, the sad-
dle horse, in the pasture and drove the black Dodge sedan up into the
foothills to check on the cattle. But I had seen enough of Pete McElprang and Miller Black and Frank Robbins to know that farmers could
be dashing horsemen, and my chief aspiration was someday to be a
farmer and stockman myself. No occupation was more esteemed in

Poplarhaven, and while Grandpa engaged in many other activities during his life he never claimed any of them as a vocation. I suppose it is from those early influences that I gained the unreflective conviction that farming is the only real work. But though several of his descendents have remained attached to the land, Grandpa was the last real farmer in our family, the last to make a living at it. By the next generation most of the men in Poplarhaven were employed as wage earners and farmed only as a sideline. Even so, the farms were more often economic liabilities than assets. As Lynn Collard used to say about his job in the coal mines, "I can't afford to be laid off. I've got a wife and kids and farm to support."

Though Grandpa's acreage was not large by current standards, it represented a consolidation of several smaller farms, each with its own history. The home field lay at the northwest corner of the townsite. Grandpa had purchased this land from Levi Harmon at the time of his marriage to Grandma, and it was here that he built his house and barnyard. The first field, a mile away at the southwest corner of town, was brought into the family by Great-grandpa Geary through a series of trades with Samuel Rowley and Abinadi Porter in the 1880s. The middle field, half a mile farther away, was the oldest of all, having been part of Great-grandpa's original homestead. The level ground had appeared to be ideal farmland, but irrigation brought alkali salts to the surface, rendering the soil unfit for anything but rough pasture. Finally there was the farther field, out in the South Flats two miles from home, the ultimate range of my early childhood explorations. Grandpa had acquired it from his stepmother, Aunt Bell, who had been holding it in the hope that her runaway son, Joseph, might someday return.

Grandpa was born in 1878 and lived for his first five years in the rock house his father had built in Round Valley, near Morgan, Utah. I have described Great-grandpa Geary as a man of great physical strength and endurance. I can barely remember him as a silent visitor sitting in the front room, but even in his old age his frame was big and strong. He died at the age of eighty-seven, the result of going to work too soon after surgery. Grandpa, however, inherited his mother's small frame and was sickly as a boy. His childhood was lonely and difficult, especially after the death of his mother when he was eight years old, and of his brother Frederick two years later, but he talked of it in a matter-of-fact way as though one could expect nothing else. One night in his teens he attended a dance after a long day in the hayfield and returned home after midnight to find his father dressed and waiting. "If you can dance, you can work," Great-grandpa said, and work they did, through the remainder of the night and all the next day. With the demands of the farm, the threshing machine, and a contract to haul freight from the railroad at Price to the Ute Indian reservation, Grandpa was never able to complete a full term of school. However, he saved enough money from his work on the freight road to attend a business college in Salt Lake City for three months, acquiring, according to the letter of recommendation he brought home with him, "such a knowledge of Bookkeeping, though he did not complete the course, that he will make a good assistant bookkeeper."

On his twenty-first birthday, Grandpa received from his father a forty-acre farm and a team of horses. With this start on a livelihood, he began courting Lauretta Wakefield, but his plans were changed by two events, a call to serve a mission for the LDS Church, and, only days before he left for the mission field, Lauretta's death from rheumatic heart disease. After serving for two years in the Northern States Mission, he returned home, received another team of horses from his father (the first team had been sold to help finance the mission), married his deceased fiancee's younger sister Alice Grace, and settled down in Poplarhaven. In addition to farming, at one time or another he worked in a bank, operated a threshing machine, served as county road supervisor, constructed roads and reservoirs, operated a general store, sold insurance, took census, and was the local correspondent for the *Deseret News*. Besides these employments, he spent twenty years as a counselor to the ward bishop plus terms as town clerk, county commissioner, school board member, irrigation company board member and secretary, and organizer of a livestock show and of a community coal mine. The range of his activities was unusual but not unique. The civic well-being of small towns has traditionally depended on a small core of able and hardworking men and women who have the confidence to tackle jobs for which they have no specific training.

Grandpa and Grandma built a two-story house of local brick, which, by the time I came along, was shaded by tall trees and looked as though it had been there forever. Our place was just through the orchard from Grandpa's, and a well-worn path ran past the big pear tree that held the treehouse and the sweet cherry with the low-hanging branch on which I tried to chin myself each time I passed.

None of the three children had wandered far from home. Aunt Fawn and Uncle Ray McCandless, after spending the early years of their marriage in the coal camps, returned to Poplarhaven to build a house across the road from Grandpa's. Uncle Merlin and Aunt Dora were the farthest away. They lived down in town, but hardly a day passed that Uncle Merlin didn't stop by for a few minutes. The whole family gathered formally at Grandpa's place on Thanksgiving and Christmas. Informally, the grandchildren congregated there daily, helping themselves to fresh bread and honey in Grandma's kitchen, playing with the marbles and blocks on the dining room floor, dressing up in the old clothes that were kept in an upstairs bedroom, enjoying a game of No Bears Are Out Tonight on summer evenings in the big yard.

Grandpa was a very early riser. The saying around town was that he had half a day's work done before most men got started. After tending the water and doing the morning chores, he would return to the house for breakfast, and sometimes, if I got up early enough, I could get there in time to share his grapefruit and tag along after him as he went on with his work. I can remember watching while he repaired harnesses and mended fence and gathered eggs. He took me with him when he went to the mill, or to Andrew Allen's blacksmith shop to get the plowshares sharpened, and, on one long, memorable day, across the mountains on a bull-buying expedition. On raw March days I played, thickly bundled, in the barn while Grandpa pitched manure in the reeking corral. When the manure spreader was full, I rode beside him on the seat as we hauled the load out to the fields. I liked best the moment when he engaged the lever that set the spreader mechanism in operation. The slatted floor moved slowly back, feeding the manure into the whirling tines that spread a brown path behind us on the still winter-bound earth.

Though not an inarticulate man (he was a frequent speaker at funerals), Grandpa had little use for idle conversation while he was working, and he liked to have me with him (I learned in later years) because I didn't chatter. We might go half a day without exchanging a dozen words, Grandpa only giving occasional succinct directions (so succinct at times that you had to know what he wanted beforehand in order to understand him) and swearing now and then at a recalcitrant piece of machinery or a cow that couldn't see an open gate. He had little patience with error and was capable of sharp rebukes, but he punished me physically only once, when I refused to divide a boiled

egg with a younger cousin and instead smashed it in my hand. I remember three things from the incident, which must have occurred
when I was four or five: the sensation of the mashed egg as it
squeezed out between my fingers; the strong conviction that I was in
the right (her brothers had eggs of their own, so why should I be the
one to share?); and the hardness of Grandpa's hand as he paddled
me. But that was the only time.

In the summer Grandpa worked outdoors early and late and fell
asleep in his chair immediately after supper. After a two-hour nap he
sleepily arose, scratched his bald head, wound the Regulator clock in
the kitchen, and climbed the stairs to bed. On winter evenings he did
the night chores in the early dark and then came inside, stamping his
feet on the porch and pausing to warm his hands at the kitchen stove.
Then, if he didn't have a meeting to go to or work to do at his oak
drop-leaf desk in the corner of the dining room, he might tell us
freight road stories.

He would tell of the time, on his first trip alone at age fourteen,
when he was frightened by an owl as he lay in his bedroll, thinking it
was someone demanding to know "Who's there? Who's there?" Or
the time when an Indian rode into his camp and demanded cake
when there was no cake, and so Grandpa had to mix up a substitute
from breadcrumbs and sugar. Or he would tell of the winter trip
when he nearly died of hypothermia before another teamster saw that
he was falling into a stupor and forced him to get down from the
wagon and run, hitting him with his whip when he tried to stop.
Then there was the time when he developed a severe cold which in-
fected his weak lungs so that he was unable to drive his outfit back
from Fort Duchesne. A young drifter of questionable reputation, a
man called "Six-shooter Bob," offered to drive the team with Grandpa lying in a makeshift bed under the wagon cover. On the way up
Nine Mile Canyon they met another party of freighters who asked
Six-shooter Bob whose team he was driving.

"Ed Geary's," he replied.

"Where's the kid?"

"Oh, he's damned sick in the wagon," Bob said. "Be dead by
the time we get to Price."

"However," Grandpa would say, "I didn't die."

As a young child I regarded Grandpa's work as my play, but as I
grew older and he expected me to take some responsibility for the
work I found it less appealing and instead of seeking him out in the

morning I would often try to avoid him. I remained fond of farming in theory, but I didn't much care for the dirt and chaff and heat of the actual labor. It annoyed me that Grandpa didn't consider that I might have other things planned for the day, that he began work too early in the morning and continued too late in the evening when I would have preferred to be out bumming with my friends. As a result of my changing attitude, Grandpa and I grew less close.

But there were still some memorable times. I can recall one day when we were harvesting grain in the middle field. I must have been about fifteen or sixteen. It was after the era of binding, shocking, hauling, and threshing. Lonnie Guymon performed all of those operations at once as he guided his big combine around the patch of oats in the one tillable corner of the field while Grandpa and I watched from our perches on the wagon. When the hopper was full, Lonnie pulled the combine out of the geometrical pattern of diminishing swaths and came bouncing across the furrows toward us. Grandpa and I held the burlap sacks up to the spout while they filled with oats then stacked them on the wagon. When the hopper was empty, the combine returned to its rounds, and we had nothing to do but sit on the full sacks and watch.

Grandpa was in a reflective mood that day. He told me about his first arrival in Poplarhaven. He could remember the long wagon trip from Arizona in minute detail: the swimming horse that almost upset the ferryboat at Lee's Ferry, the old Danish woman who wandered away from camp and got lost in the Kaibab Forest, the pitcherful of honey that his father purchased at a ranch in Johnson Canyon. He pointed out the notch in the Blue Ridge from which they had caught their first sight of Poplarhaven. His father had stopped the wagons there while they viewed the cabins that were spread across the treeless flat. Grandpa remembered that his mother cried when his father told them that this was their new home. They lived in the wagon boxes until his father could build a one-room cabin, which was furnished, he remembered, with a Charter Oak cookstove, a wooden bedstead, a wash bench, a looking glass, a Woodbury clock, a rocking chair and four straight-backed chairs, a cradle, and a wheat bin in a corner. He remembered that his mother was never well after the birth of Maud Maryann and remarked that perhaps she would have lived if there had been a doctor. He recalled the death of Frederick, his closest playmate. His father had awakened him in the night to say that Fred was dying and to send him to fetch a neighbor woman to lay out the body. A few years later, as a boy of twelve, he had been in this very field, getting the horses to take his stepmother to the doctor in Price, when a man rode out from town to tell him not to bother, that she was already dead. He went on to talk of the long series of house-keepers and hired girls that passed through their home before his father finally married Aunt Bell, a witty and sensible English widow. "Her entry into our home made living conditions much better," Grandpa said.

Grandpa's heart failed in his last years, and he had to depend increasingly on others to do the work on the farm. But he continued to push himself for as long as he could. I can remember watching him stagger out to tend the water, shovel perched on his bony shoulder, and having horrific visions of him dying in the field before he could make it back to the house. It didn't occur to me then that that would have suited him better than a lingering death in bed. Finally he grew so weak that he had to stay in the house, often with an oxygen tube in his mouth.

I remember one day that summer when I was raking the hay into windrows. It had been a bad day, with several breakdowns of the machinery, and the job was still unfinished by late afternoon. I knew how Grandpa felt about getting the hay raked before it got too dry. (He was always suspicious of the side-delivery rake in any case, feeling that it knocked off more leaves than the old horse-drawn dump rake.) But I was tired and frustrated, and I had plans for the evening, so I drove the tractor in from the field as fast as it would go, jerked to a stop in the yard, and jumped off and started through the orchard for home. Before I had gone halfway up the path, I heard the creak of the gate and turned to look. It was Grandpa, shuffling painfully across the yard toward the tractor, going to finish the job.

FIVE

Memorable Conflagrations
of My Early Years

In the early days the meetinghouse bell served as an all-purpose
public timepiece and alarm, ringing half an hour before meeting on
Sundays and for fires and other emergencies at any time. Later a siren
was installed on the drugstore roof, and that was the full extent of the
firefighting apparatus in Poplarhaven during most of my childhood.
There was no question of putting a fire out once it had started. When
you heard the siren, you ran outside and looked around for the
smoke. Eventually somebody thought up a more organized scheme,
and the siren sounded a different number of wails for each quarter of
the town. The earlier system was generally adequate, though, because
by the time the siren blew the fire was usually well along and the
smoke was visible from anywhere in town.

A fire was a public spectacle and social event in Poplarhaven.
Our most exciting times were when we got together to watch somebody's house burn down. Men would leave their teams in the field,
women their dishes in the pan or pears half-peeled, and we would all
congregate at the scene of the fire. Women and children stood back at
a safe distance while the men and older boys entered the burning
structure to save what they could, lugging out dressers and beds and
sofas and armloads of dishes, all of which were placed in a heap on
the front lawn. It was a scary thing to watch a father or uncle or cousin
disappear into a burning house, leaving you with visions of collapsing
stairs and crumbling walls. The anxiety mounted with every second
until he finally emerged carrying some absurdly trivial object to
deposit on the growing pile before he ran back inside again.

Soon the time came when no one would enter the house. What
could be saved had been saved, and we all stood back, our duty done,
to watch the climax. By now the flames would have broken through
the roof, throwing an orange glare on the towering column of smoke.
The anticipation mounted until suddenly—always before you quite

expected it—the roof fell in with a great roar and a mass of cinders soared skyward, accompanied by a long-drawn-out "Oooh!" from the spectators.

It was soon over after that. In an incredibly short time a structure that had seemed to hold a permanent place in the town was reduced to a few pieces of charred timber, a cookstove standing forlornly where the kitchen had been, and a foundation that appeared far too small for the house that had once stood on it.

Before the embers cooled, a new round of activity had begun. The bishop would be gathering up the displaced family and arranging temporary lodgings while the Relief Society president was taking an inventory of their immediate needs, dipping into the storehouse for bedding and starting a fund-raising drive to replace the furniture not saved from the flames. Sometimes a family could even come out ahead after a burnout. That happened when the Colfaxes lost their home, one cold night just before Christmas. The Colfaxes were a numerous family who lived in a log house dating from the first years of the settlement, to which they had added shanty wings of unpainted lumber. The whole thing went up almost instantaneously. By the time we reached the scene, the roof had already fallen in, and the family, some still in their nightclothes, were standing forlornly in the snow. They had saved nothing.

They didn't have much to save in any case. They were extremely poor and had a child in almost every grade in school plus several preschoolers, shy, backward children who were despised by the other kids. The fire changed that, at least to some extent. I suppose there is a lasting trauma that comes from seeing your home burn, and there may well have been some sentimental treasures among the small store of material goods they lost. But to an outside observer it appeared that their standard of living and their morale both took a turn for the better after the fire. The bishop found them a better house to live in, and the hand-me-down clothes collected for the children were an improvement on their usual attire. They seemed to become more outgoing and to be better accepted at school. Perhaps they didn't actually change. Perhaps it was just that having their plight brought dramatically to our attention, and having invested some of our own substance in their rehabilitation, we began to regard them in a new light.

With so many fires to watch, we became almost connoisseurs, able to determine the quality of the blaze from the first glimpse of smoke. Light smoke meant a haystack fire, very commonplace and not very exciting unless it should happen to spread. A black pillar of smoke meant that a house was on fire, but even then there were distinctions. The old log and plank dwellings, their unpainted wood aged for decades in the dry climate, went up like tinder. Adobe and brick houses burned only on the inside, of course, but there was always the question of whether the walls would fall when the floors collapsed. Usually they did, at least on the upper story. Many of the finest houses burned down. Evidently there had been some flaw in the construction that made the brick houses built in the 1890s especially vulnerable to chimney fires. That is the reason why the fires often occurred in the winter, when the stoves were hottest. Another plentiful fire season was the late summer and fall, canning season, when overheated cookstoves ignited many a house.

My grandfather had difficulty sleeping in his last years. He would occupy the long watches of the night by making mental lists of various things: widows, missionaries who had gone out from the Poplarhaven Ward, funerals he had spoken at, families who had moved away, and houses he had seen burn down. He tallied some sixty of these, in addition to the really big fires, such as the one that destroyed the old log meetinghouse in 1918, or the one that burned the schoolhouse in 1923, or the forest fire of 1938 that lasted for the better part of a week. He didn't even count the barns and haystacks he had seen destroyed.

I cannot match Grandpa's catalog of fires, but I could make up a sizeable list. At the head of the list—the first fire I can remember and the one that came closest to burning us out—is the burning of the Brasher Hotel. It was one of the great fires in Poplarhaven, and one of the very few cases in which something that could have burned down did not.

I was only two years old at the time, and we lived in a three-room apartment over Grandpa's store. To get there, you had to climb a steep, narrow stairway that was rather scary, but once you reached our living quarters they were quite satisfactory. From the front room windows, I had a fine view of Poplarhaven's two-block "downtown," from the high school and the meetinghouse on the south to the drugstore and Dr. Hill's office on the north. I was fascinated by the coming and going of cars on Main Street and by the way they parked in front of the stores and public buildings. I spent hours playing "meeting," which meant that I moved my toy cars back and forth from the sofa to the chair, carefully parking them at a forty-five-degree angle.

Grandpa's store and the hotel stood side by side, two frame buildings separated by only a few inches and a thin sheet metal firewall. Grandpa and Reub Brasher had always said that if one of the buildings ever caught fire they would both surely burn down. The fire started while Ivie Brasher and her girls were bottling peaches at the end of the summer. My parents were out of town, attending some pre-school meetings in Green River, and I was staying with my grandparents. They took me downtown with them to see what could be saved. As usual, there was a good turnout to watch the fire, and willing hands hauled our possessions down the narrow stairway and piled them in a heap across the road. The only mishap occurred when somebody tossed the box containing Mother's china from the upstairs porch instead of carrying it down the stairs. I stood beside the growing pile of goods yelling, "Don't forget the corn flakes!" until somebody finally took me across the square to Aunt Irene's house, where they let me play in a drawer full of odd buttons until I fell asleep.

My parents had received a telephone call in Green River, informing them that both the hotel and the store had burned to the ground. They made the two-hour drive back to Poplarhaven with that image before them, and as they entered town Mother said, "What if it were still standing?" And it was, still untouched beside the rubble of the hotel. We didn't move back into it, but it stood throughout my youth, serving as our school lunchroom, and when Uncle Merlin tore it down at last the old building proved to be so firmly put together that he could scarcely take it apart.

Besides our accidental fires, we had the annual spring fires. Poplarhaven was built on saltgrass flats, and the early spring, before the new growth started, was the best time to burn the rough old grass along the ditchbanks. In addition, some farmers set fire to their pastures, believing that burning off the old growth not only allowed the new shoots to grow more freely but actually supplied valuable nutrients. One spring when Clee Larkin was burning his pasture, which was behind his house in the middle of town, on the same block as most of the stores, the wind shifted, and it looked for a while as though the whole business district might go. The fire got going just as school was letting out for the day, and of course we all hurried to the scene—all but Allen Litster, who veered off towards the meeting-house because it was Primary day. (He came out all right, though. Since nobody else showed up, they had to cancel Primary, and he got to watch the fire with a clear conscience.)

As it turned out, the fire destroyed nothing but an empty chicken coop, but it was very exciting for a while. When the flames had died down and we were breaking up to go home, we got one last unexpected bit of fun. The fire engine from Price came wailing into town, having come twenty miles on the news that Poplarhaven was burning down. It was a good day.

The next spring when Clee burned his pasture, a spark got into his haystack and he lost his whole corral. When he could see that it was getting out of hand, he threw open the gate and gave the brindle milk cow a kick in the belly that sent her running out of the yard. It took Clee's wife two days to find her. Then she sold her to Uncle Ray for seventy-five dollars. After that, Clee let the saltgrass grow.

SIX

Hying to Kolob

Bishop Heber Leonard used to insist that the spirit world was right here on earth and the dead were never far from home. He was not really the bishop anymore, but the title was for life and carried, to my young mind, an immense weight of dignity and authority. I remember the quivering of his beard as he talked about the spirit world in some otherwise long forgotten church meeting. The dead were all around us, he said, some of them right there in the meetinghouse at that very moment, but we couldn't see them because of the veil. When you were about to die, the veil would open up and you would see your parents or wife or whoever you had on the other side. But Brother Crandall, who was equal to Bishop Leonard in age and dignity though without title or beard, maintained that when the spirit left the body it traveled in the twinkling of an eye to distant Kolob, the planet nearest to the throne of God, where it remained either in paradise or in spirit prison until the resurrection day. Only the righteous, he said, those worthy to inherit the celestial kingdom, would return to the earth after it had been cleansed and renewed.

When Bishop Leonard and Brother Crandall differed on a point of doctrine, as they often did, they debated with great vigor, quoting scripture and prophets and resonant phrases such as "paradisiacal glory" and "weeping and wailing and gnashing of teeth." Brother Crandall clearly had the more epic vision of life after death, but I preferred Bishop Leonard's view with its suggestion of a comfortable continuity between this world and the next. It seemed to me that a spirit would be better off in familiar surroundings than in some strange new place, even if it was paradise. Of spirit prison I hardly dared to think. Besides, if the earth was to be renewed and receive its paradisiacal glory, why should the spirits have to go hying all over the universe? Wouldn't it make more sense, when the graves were thrown open on resurrection morning, to have them simply take up their bodies and go on about their business?

The earth to me then meant our wide valley in the shelter of the plateau, and the town that lay, like the New Jerusalem, foursquare on the land, its length the same as its breadth. But instead of walls we had straight rows of lombardy poplars; instead of jeweled buildings there were houses of buff-colored brick set deep in shady yards, and weathered barns crammed with hay, all in all a pleasanter place, I thought, than the city described by St. John.

We lived on the most interesting side of town, close to the public corral, the mill, Sandberg's Hill, and the graveyard. The graveyard, which was more populous than the town, was just over a low ridge from our home, out of sight yet within easy walking distance. My interest in the place dated from the death of my great-grandfather when I was five. His passing brought no sense of loss, for I knew him only as an occasional silent visitor in dark glasses, sitting in the padded rocking chair in Grandpa's front room. It was not the death that impressed me but the funeral and the burial. As we filed past the coffin, where it stood banked with flowers at the front of the meetinghouse, my father lifted me up so that I could see inside. Great-grandpa lay there not so much stiller than I remembered him but pale and oddly dressed in a white cap and white robe with a green apron. Mother whispered something about temple clothes, and I nodded as though I understood. The coffin lid was left open throughout the funeral service, perhaps, I thought, so Great-grandpa could hear the talks. If he listened he was apparently not displeased, though unmoved. Nor did he protest when, at the end of the funeral, the lid was closed and the coffin carried out to the hearse. I remember the dusty parade to the graveyard, and Grandpa's praying over the grave that the mortal remains might rest undisturbed until the morning of the first resurrection. Then the undertaker pressed a lever, and the coffin sank smoothly into the straight-sided hole. I remember with a special clarity how straight and clean-cut the sides of the grave were, like the walls of a house, or rather, since the grave was so narrow, like a hallway leading from one room to another, perhaps a part of a great subterranean mansion whose dim, cool chambers stretched on and on.

For some time after that I looked for someone else to die so we could have another funeral. Great-grandpa Geary had died of old age, and there were lots of old people around: old Mr. Sandberg who lived by the mill and walked with a cane and was deaf; Bert Westover whose house was across the road from Grandpa's and who was bent with rheumatism; Mrs. Johnson who hobbled up the road every day or two to visit Grandma, arriving red-faced and panting and saying, as she settled into the rocking chair, "Lard, I'm going to drop dead in the road someday." If she did, somebody would have to pick her up and dress her in white clothes before they could have a funeral. Even Grandpa and Grandma were old, though not as old as Great-grandpa since he was Grandpa's father. The skin on the back of Grandpa's hands was like thin brown leather, and Grandma, when she had worked too hard, would press her hand against her side and say that she was about out of breath. You could die, I knew, from running out of breath, and also from car wrecks or from getting very sick, or you could be killed in the war.

There were other deaths, other funerals, other dusty processions to the graveyard, but they didn't have much bearing on my own life until my ninth summer, the summer the headstone man came. There was an outbreak of polio that year, and several people from Poplarhaven and the surrounding towns contracted the disease. There were three or four deaths, including a girl I knew. I had seen her in Sunday School just a few days before she died. She had seemed quite normal then, as healthy as I was, but by the next Sunday she was dead. I didn't attend the funeral, but I walked over to the graveyard towards evening and looked at the short mound of blue-gray earth covered with bright wreaths.

When Great-grandpa Geary died it had been interesting but not threatening. He seemed safely remote from my own life. But this girl was younger than I, and yet she had died. I had heard my parents discuss the progress of her disease, and I was aware that they were unusually solicitous of my health. They forbade me to go swimming in the creek or even wading in the canal. So it could happen to me too; there was no special exemption on my account. As that appalling realization struck home, I began to be morbidly aware of my bodily functions. At frequent intervals, I took mental inventory of the rate of my breathing, the elevation of my temperature, virtually the beating of my heart. When I woke up in the morning, I immediately felt my forehead to see if it was hot and swallowed hard to test whether my throat was sore. During the day I would suddenly realize that I had not been thinking about my health, and I would anxiously check again. Sometimes I swallowed so hard and so often, making sure that I still could, that my throat did begin to feel sore. Then I became terrified and avoided my parents lest they should discover that I was ill and take me to the doctor, thereby confirming the awful fact.

Though my fears began with polio, they did not end there. I worried about getting every disease I had heard of, cancer, diphtheria, scarlet fever. My organism came to seem so vulnerable that I doubted its ability to maintain itself even in the absence of infection. When my heart beat rapidly in my chest after exercise, I grew alarmed that it might burst or wear out. At night, on the verge of sleep, I would suddenly realize that I couldn't remember my last breath, and would fill my lungs again and again until it made me light-headed. Then I would lie awake worrying that I might stop breathing in my sleep when I didn't know about it.

It was while I was in the midst of these anxieties that the head-stone man came to town. He arrived late one afternoon in a large gray van which he parked in the shade of the cottonwood trees just across the canal from Grandpa's place. The van had a bunk and cookstove inside, like a sheepherder's wagon, in addition to the stoneworking tools and some slabs of polished granite. The headstone man was as gray as his van, a fine gray dust covering his clothes, his skin, his grizzled hair. He drove to the graveyard each day, where most of his work was replacing broken stones. Then in the evenings he came back and parked under the cottonwoods. He bought eggs and butter from Grandma and got his water from Grandpa's hydrant.

There were many such itinerant craftsmen in those days, piano tuners, photographers, scissors grinders, who stayed for a day or a week in one town then moved on to another through a wide circuit of rural Utah. Most of them passed through and were forgotten, but the headstone man stayed for several weeks and I got to know him fairly well. I often accompanied him to the graveyard, watching as he dug out the old stone and prepared a foundation for the new, sometimes helping him by carrying water from the tap for the concrete that he mixed in a low trough. I felt safe with him since he was friendly but still a stranger, not likely to inquire too closely into my health or bundle me off to the doctor. And then his profession fit in with my fascination with death. I had a fancy, which had originated at Great-grandpa Geary's burial, that the headstones might conceal an entrance to the grave. It seemed reasonable that the larger ones, at least, might open up in some secret way and reveal a flight of steps descending into the ground, rather like Grandpa's cellar stairs. Such an image lessened the finality of death, suggested the possibility of coming and going, made of the grave a sort of home. There was a family story that when Great-grandpa Olsen felt himself growing old he went to the carpenter and ordered a double-wide coffin so that he would have room to turn over if he wanted to. He kept it in a shed behind his house until he died, and used to show it to visitors when they came to call. I too liked the idea of having some room to move around, but I preferred to think of underground chambers connected to one another, where there was no confinement but rather a secret subterranean life. The cellar was my prototype, snug from the weather and smelling of damp earth and rotting timbers and last year's apples. You could live in a place like a cellar, I thought. Only you would want to have a light.

It is hard to say why I found this fantasy so compelling. I was aware of the church's teachings on life after death and could have explained, if asked, that only the body was buried in the ground while the spirit went to the spirit world. But the spirit world had to be someplace, and since I had no desire to hie to Kolob when I died I preferred to think, with Bishop Leonard, that it was here on earth. And why not at the graveyard, where the rows of headstones told of bodies resting below the ground, awaiting resurrection? But even the most comforting thought of the hereafter was disquieting to me. In all my prayers I asked that I might not get polio or any other disease but might grow up and fulfill my earthly mission. That was a reassuring phrase I had picked up at church. The Lord would protect you, if you were righteous, until you had fulfilled your earthly mission. Of course, when people died young it was said that their earthly mission was finished and they were needed on the other side. But I felt sure that there was no pressing need for me on the other side and that I had a good long earthly mission to fulfill that would carry me—if I didn't get polio or stop breathing in my sleep—well into the years of manhood and beyond the fear of death. Perhaps, indeed, there was no necessity for me to die at all. I had heard of the Three Nephites, who had been permitted to remain on earth until the Second Coming. They stayed alive century after century, going about the earth doing good deeds. I would be willing to do good deeds if I could live on like that. Gradually in my prayers, especially when I went into the willow patch by the canal and offered up my petitions vocally and without restraint, I began asking, not merely to escape the polio epidemic, or even to grow up, but to stay alive forever. For if the spirit and the body were to be reunited on resurrection day, why should they have to be separated at all? As my prayer took shape through repetition, my confidence grew that my earthly mission was to be unending. It seemed as though my soul had a special harmony with the living earth that precluded dissolution. Sometimes I felt that I was already immortal. Nevertheless, whenever my head felt feverish or my throat sore, my chest would tighten with fear and dread.

Sometimes, while we waited for a concrete footing to harden, the headstone man and I wandered through the graveyard, and he gave me the benefit of his professional observations. In the oldest section, some graves were marked with common sandstone from the nearby hills, with names and dates scratched in with a knife, and some merely had wooden planks planted in the ground like a post, so rotten that they would break off at the slightest push.

"The families done these theirselves," the headstone man said. "In the early days they had to make do."

He pointed out the succession of markers from the crude pioneer stones through the cream-colored Manti limestone and the cast iron to the newer marbles and granites.

"This here don't weather good enough for a monument," he said of the limestone, rubbing the surface and showing me a fine granular powder on his hand. "They used a lot of it, though, before they could afford marble or granite from back East. My father done a lot of work in limestone."

The newer stones were richly polished but plain, with simple inscriptions, but some of the limestone slabs bore intricate decorations. Some identified handcart pioneers, or listed the towns that the dead person had helped to settle. Two that I had thought were for soldiers, even though they didn't have flagpoles, were actually on the graves of missionaries who had died in the field. "Soldiers of the Lord," the headstone man said. The lambs on children's graves and the doves were designs brought over from Denmark, where his father had learned the trade. Other designs were original to Utah, such as the open Book of Mormon, or the sego lilies, replicas of the fragile, porcelain-like flowers that I never picked when I found them on the hills, since they had saved the pioneers from starvation and were the state flower. The headstone man pointed out the clasped hands carved on several stones and a rather spooky looking eye that stared blankly from the top of an obelisk. "Those are temple signs," he said, and wagged his head significantly. I didn't understand him, but at the mention of the temple and with the image before me of a single, unflickering eye staring down as though from distant Kolob, I began to sense the presence of an obscure network of signs and symbols that linked the seen and unseen worlds.

At the top of the graveyard we found a large stone with an elaborate cluster of roofs and towers carved on it, which the headstone man identified as the Celestial City. "It took Father days to do one of those," he said, "but they was his favorites. While he carved, he used to tell me about how the Saints would dwell there all arrayed in spotless white. You see," he continued after a pause, "these things wasn't just for decoration. There's a meaning to them. But there ain't much call for this sort of work anymore. Folks won't stand the expense."

At day's end, the headstone man often brought out an old spindle-legged chair and sat by the canal. Sometimes Bert Westover came over to squat on his heels and jaw for a spell. When I could slip out of the house after supper, I would join them there, gathering apricots on the way from the tree that spread over the cellar. I climbed onto the cellar roof to reach the laden branches and carried the fruit in my shirt. Then I would sprawl on the ditchbank and watch the spasmodic motions of the water striders while I listened to the men talk.

Bert Westover was one of the most vivid characters of my childhood, a dry, shrunken old man with widely bowed legs. He had a farm up the road toward the canyon, but he raised little on it, only a few acres of hay for his horses. The horses were his only livestock. There were ten or twelve of them, and for all practical purposes they belonged to the whole neighborhood. They grazed freely along the ditchbanks, and if we ever failed to close a gate they were sure to get into our fields and gardens. Once in a while, Iver Truman would spot promise in one of Bert's colts, and they would groom it for the races, hoping they had found a successor to the legendary Kelton, Iver's racehorse of the 1920s. For the most part, though, the horses, like their owner, lived lives of boundless leisure, though by his own account Bert Westover had had an adventurous career. Whenever he got a chance to talk, he settled slowly onto his heels, legs spread apart and arms draped across his thighs in an easy equilibrium strangely out of keeping with the stiffness of his movements. Then he automatically reached into his left breast pocket to fish out his sack of Bull Durham by the orange tab on the drawstring. With unbroken concentration, he spread the mouth of the sack and shook a little of the brown leaf into a white tissue held just so between his fingers. Then, his hands trembling slightly all the while, he leveled it judiciously and folded up the sides, gave a quick motion of his tongue to moisten the joint, twisted the ends, and stuck the cigarette in his mouth. Then came an awkward fumbling for a match before he could draw the first deep breath and begin to talk.

"Well," he drawled, "you're in a good line, ain't you? As long as folks keep dying."

The headstone man would nod agreeably. "Surest thing in the world," he said, tilting his chair back against the side of the van.

"Course you'll be out of a job come resurrection day." Bert Westover paused to draw on his cigarette or spit into the canal, the yellowish bubbles drifting lightly on the water until they hit a rapid stretch and disintegrated. "Hell of a time that'll be, people crawling out of the ground like salamanders in a mud puddle. I figure to move away from here before then. Mine's the first place they'll hit when they come over the hill, and they'll eat me out of house and home."

Bert Westover's house was a weathered plank cabin. When old Sister Westover, Bert's mother, was alive, Grandma said, it was a nice little house with floorboards scrubbed and curtains on the windows. But Bert, being an old batch, had abandoned all but the front room where he had an iron bedstead in one corner and a cookstove in another. Suckers from the yellow rose at the rear of the house had grown up through the floor of the back room and pressed against the window to reach the light.

"The men come first, ain't that right? Then they call up their wives. Joe Miller says his old lady will wait a hell of a long while in that old blue clay before he calls her up. Says it'll be the first time he's ever had her where he wanted her.''

One evening Bert told of digging up a mummified Indian years before, when he was working on the county road. "He was all folded up till he wasn't no longer than that," he said, holding his hands three feet apart. "Smart way of burying. You don't need such a big hole.''

The headstone man pursed his lips in professional disapproval, but Bert had found a line of talk he wanted to pursue. "Tough job getting the kinks out on resurrection day, though.'' He spat again. "Naw, when you've dug up a corpse or two, you can't swallow the resurrection business. When you're dead you're dead.''

"Careful," the headstone man said quietly. "The boy.''

Bert Westover went to join the people in the graveyard a few years later, long before they had a chance to descend on his house for their resurrection breakfast. When I was a teenager, we used to take girls to his cabin on Halloween to scare them. The headstone man was past his middle years then and no doubt has a headstone of his own by now. Grandma, in spite of her weak heart, outlived both Grandpa and Dad, who died just a year apart while I was in college. It amazes me to think that I am now as old as my father was when he died. Sometimes, now, it seems as though Bishop Leonard was right and they are just across a veil, but sometimes I sense with Brother Crandall that they are immensely far away, as far as Kolob.

One day, near the end of the headstone man's stay, Grandpa and Dad and I went with him to the graveyard to replace the broken limestone monument on Aunt Anna's grave. Dad dug out the old stone and widened the hole for the foundation, and I carried water to mix the concrete. After the soft gray mud was poured, Grandpa took the shovel over to Great-grandpa's grave, where the settling of the earth had left a depression. He filled in the low spot and carefully leveled it off even with the surrounding ground, then stood leaning on the shovel.

"I suppose that's where you'll put Grace and me," he said, indicating a space beside Great-grandpa's grave.

When the job was finished, Grandpa rode home with the headstone man, but Dad and I walked, taking the long way over Sandberg's Hill. Dad told me the names he had given to each of the ridges and hollows when he had played on the hill as a boy. It struck me as odd because I called them by different names; yet they were the same places. It was strange to think of my father as a boy and of Grandpa as a boy before him. And in all that time the hills hadn't changed. It was only people who changed, grew up, had children of their own, grew old, and died. I began to catch a vision of mortality, of mutability, that went beyond the mere anxiety about my own death, though its outlines remained vague. It had something to do with the permanence of the earth and the transience of all who dwelt upon it. When we descended from the hill, we walked past the mill where old Mr. Sandberg, sitting on the porch, waved his cane at us and called out a greeting in his high-pitched voice. He talked that way because he couldn't hear. The noisy machinery in the mill had made him deaf.

After we reached home, I slipped away and sought out my secret place in the willows. There I fell to my knees and shut my eyes but for several minutes formed no words. When the prayer came, it began as so many others had done that summer, with the petition that I might not die. But now it was not the imminent threat of polio or early death that impelled me but rather the general weight of mortality. I knew that merely my own exemption from the common fate was not enough. To live on, unchanged, while the others changed and failed and died would be terrible. I saw in my mind an empty house and abandoned sheds and the cellar with its roof caved in, like a grave. For the first time I thought of the Three Nephites as lonely, living on and on with all of their people gone. So I prayed that my parents and grandparents and brother and sister might also live forever, unchanged from what they were at that moment. I thought of Bert Westover and Mr. and Mrs. Sandberg, but I sensed that it was unwise to ask too much of the Lord. Probably not everyone could stay alive forever, and I reluctantly surrendered the upper floors of the mill where Mr. Sandberg was my guide. Anyway, maybe on the other side he would be able to hear again, so it might be better for him. But other problems presented themselves. What about my mother's father, the grandfather I had never known, who was already dead? And what about my grandparents' parents? Wouldn't they miss them if they stayed alive forever? Emboldened by my need, I prayed that they might be made alive again and remain forever too, but even as I named them a wave of futility swept over me, for where could it end?

Great-grandpa had had a mother and father too, and they, and they. I saw a horde of strangers, each linked to those beside them but alien to the rest, marching over the hill and filling the house, the yard.

No, it was clearly impossible. I stopped praying and remained in frustrated silence for a time then got slowly to my feet. I stepped out of the willows into the slanting light of late afternoon and cut through Grandpa's yard toward the headstone man's camp. The shadows of the cottonwoods covered the gray van and stretched across the road to Bert Westover's cabin. On this side, the sun still shone on the apricot tree beside the cellar, and I could see a few fruits, the last of the season, still hanging on the upper branches. They were too high to reach from the cellar roof. If I wanted them I would have to climb.

II

SEVEN

Why I Believe in Santa Claus

In late November each year, the town marshall hung the five or six strands of colored lights across Main Street, and Clare Guymon put a few toys out on the counter at his store. The turkeys and pilgrim hats came down from the schoolroom walls, and the teachers brought out the red and green construction paper to make Christmas chains. On a bright Saturday in early December, Dad would pack us into the car and drive up the canyon in quest of a Christmas tree. We trailed behind him in the snow from tree to tree, examining each one from every angle until we either found a perfect specimen or got too cold to continue. Back home, he hammered a wooden stand to the base while Mother brought the lights and foil icicles out of the closet and lifted down from the high shelf the box containing the fragile glass balls that seemed to hold an entire world in their brilliant depths.

Though I welcomed these preparations, they did not for a moment delude me into thinking that Christmas could be brought to pass by mere mortal efforts. There was just too much that clearly smacked of the miraculous. For example, there were the Christmas catalogs that suddenly appeared one day in everybody's box at the post office. Though they bore the names of Sears, Roebuck, and Gumpy Wards, it was obvious they had come straight from the North Pole. No store could possibly have contained such an abundance of barnyards and soda fountains and Erector Sets with real motors. It seemed incredible to me that with such clear evidence some kids at school still doubted the existence of Santa Claus.

But my faith was based on something even more certain than a Christmas catalog. I had met Santa in person. Not just a "helper," mind you, but Santa Claus himself. It happened at a Sunday School Christmas party in the old meetinghouse. He was there to hand out little brown paper bags full of goodies, tangible promises of better things to come on Christmas Eve. After he had completed the distribution and had swept out of the building in a torrent of "ho-ho-ho's" and a jingle of bells, my father suddenly suggested that we go out and see the sleigh and reindeer. We made the mistake of using the front door instead of following Santa through the side exit, and by the time we turned the corner of the building Santa was gone. It was too bad that Dad didn't get the idea sooner. I would have been willing to forego my sackful of peanuts and hardtack in order to wait outside by the sleigh and watch Santa take off. In fact, I made up my mind to do just that the next year. Unfortunately, Santa must have been at Castle Dale or Orangeville when the next Christmas party rolled around because all we had was Cliff Howard in a red suit.

While I never doubted the existence of Santa Claus, there were some things about him that were hard to figure out. For example, there was the difficulty of clear communication. After you had pored over the catalogs and painfully narrowed your requests down to a reasonable number (for if Santa thought you were being greedy he was likely to bring you nothing at all), you had to compose a letter setting forth the desires of your heart in proper form. Then, since there was apparently no regular postal service to the North Pole in those days, you put the letter, carefully addressed, into the stove. The theory was that the ashes would fly up the chimney and find their way to Santa. It seemed to be a fairly good system but not a perfect one. My requests for an electric train, in particular, seemed to get garbled in transmission. The first time I asked for an electric train, I got a wind-up one instead.

"Maybe Santa thought you weren't old enough," Mother said.

The next year, when the requested train again failed to materialize, she said, "Maybe Santa thought you were too old."

Another thing that troubled me was Santa's abrupt shifts in behavior. Before Christmas he could be very open and friendly, as he was at the Sunday School party. Yet on Christmas Eve he was so extremely secretive that to catch him at work would be disastrous. Nor was it enough merely to wait quietly in your bedroom while he made his delivery. You had to be asleep, or else he wouldn't come at all. My mother had told me of a Christmas in her childhood when, unable to go to sleep, she had heard Santa's sleigh bells coming up the road. Aware that he had a way of knowing if anyone was awake in the house, she had by sheer force of will made herself fall asleep before the bells arrived. It was a close call and a terrifying story to me because I knew I could never go to sleep in such circumstances.

I couldn't go to sleep on Christmas Eve under any circumstances. As soon as we had pinned our stockings to the side of the green chair (it was the only time I didn't resent the fact that my parents made me wear long cotton stockings in the winter, held up with garters like a girl's) and set out a plateful of cookies or applesauce cake and a glass of milk for Santa's refreshment, I would jump into bed, long before my usual bedtime, in the hope that sleeping would make the night go by faster. The cold sheets were deliciously stimulating, and I would snuggle deep into them and fill my brain with Christmas thoughts to waft me to dreamland. Pretty soon, though, the sheets would grow too warm, and I tossed this way and that in the bed to find a cool spot. Finally, I would doze off and awaken, sure that it must be almost morning, only to discover that scarcely fifteen minutes had passed since I had last looked at the clock. The clock must have stopped, then. But no, it was still ticking regularly. When my rumpled bed had grown intolerable, I would get up and go to the window, gazing out into the peculiar brilliance that seemed to characterize Christmas Eves in those days. In such crystalline air a flying sleigh would be visible for a long way. I wondered whether Santa would fly up from the other end of town, hopping from house to house, or whether he would sweep in from the west across the snow-covered fields. Sometimes I opened the window and drank in the icy air as I listened for the distant sound of bells.

The night seemed interminable as I dozed and tossed and dozed and tossed. It seemed as though I hardly slept at all, yet somehow I was always asleep when Santa came. When the clock finally said four-thirty or five, I crept down the stairs and peered into the front room to see dim shapes that had not been there the night before.

"He's come!" I shouted as I routed out the other kids. Mother and Dad would emerge from their bedroom blinking sleepily and asking what time it was, so tired that they didn't even seem surprised at what Santa had brought.

Mother used to maintain, when I woke her up on Christmas morning, that Santa's great personal treat was to spend the entire day sleeping after his night-long rounds. I doubted that. Surely the folks at the North Pole would not waste the glorious day in sleeping after preparing for a whole year. I thought of them as spending Christmas Day much as we did when we played with our toys through the early hours and then, about midmorning, made our way down the orchard path to Grandpa's place for the family gathering. I could envision the elves mingling in the warm, crowded rooms, admiring one another's toys. Mrs. Santa and her helpers would be bustling around the kitchen the way Grandma and Mother and Aunt Fawn and Aunt Dora did, trying to keep out of each other's way as they mashed the potatoes and stirred the gravy on the big coal range or whipped cream for the fruit salad or made the rich white sauce for the date pudding. Then at last when everything was ready and the dining room table had been stretched out to its fullest extent, everyone would gather round for the feast. Santa Claus himself—who, like Grandpa, had been perhaps a little detached from the activity, had been out doing chores, no doubt, throwing down some hay from the barn for the tired reindeer—would pull his captain's chair up to the head of the table, look around at the gathered clan, and scratch his bald spot. Then he would bow his head and speak the few words that brought the whole chaotic, rich occasion into focus, making it an object to be preserved in the memory as one might keep a shining glass Christmas tree ornament, untarnished all through the years.

EIGHT

Winter Chores

Chores are no respecters of occasions. When I speak of chores, I don't mean the odd household tasks that commonly go by that name in urban life, and which can usually be fitted into odd moments of the day or the week. I mean farm chores, the water to be tended, stock to be fed, cows to be milked, eggs to be gathered twice a day, weekdays and Sundays, summers and (except for tending water) winters. It doesn't matter whether it is the Fourth of July or Christmas or the night of the junior prom. Chores have to be done. A grave illness, a death in the family, an emotional crisis, and it may seem as though nothing else matters, but the chores are still there morning and night. If you knew the world was going to end tomorrow, you would still have to milk the cow tonight. Chores are what you have to do whether you want to or not.

Except for their oppressive regularity, though, chores are not necessarily unpleasant. Indeed, there is no better way to start a summer day than with morning chores. No matter how early you begin, you rise to a world already active: meadowlarks singing on the fenceposts, pigs snuffling expectantly at the trough, chickens cackling over their eggs. The walk to the top of the field to tend water is delightful, with the smell of the dew, the vistas of cropland and fenceline and boundary tree and blue mountain, the sudden explosion of a pheasant and its crowing, wing-beating flight followed by the long smooth glide to earth. Even milking Old Jers is tolerable when she comes in clean from the pasture. You sit with your head resting against her dappled flank, your wrists flexing rhythmically as the twin streams flow into the foamy bucket. A few feet away, the cats sit eagerly waiting for a warm squirt aimed in their direction. At the end, you will carry the full bucket to the kitchen and run the milk through the strainer into the enameled pans to let the cream rise. That is one of the permanent images of abundance for me.

But winter chores are another matter, especially winter morning chores in the frigid mountain valleys. It is so painfully early when you have to get up. Bundled to the ears, you step from the house into a region more cold and black than the depths of outer space. Milk bucket slung over your arm, you let your feet follow the familiar unseen path until, at the barn door, you reach instinctively for the switch that turns on the yard light. Its sudden glare hollows out a space in the darkness but gives no warmth. You blink in the light and shiver and hurry to the tasks that must be done.

The coldest object I have ever touched is a pitchfork handle in the January pre-dawn. It is a cold against which gloves give no protection, a cold that penetrates your hands and conveys an ache to your very core. Your arms feel brittle with it as you tug the forkfuls of hay from the stack and carry them to the manger. You hammer with a heel at the ice-covered water trough, then turn on the hydrant to fill a bucket for the chickens. If the hydrant is frozen, it is back to the house for a bucket of hot water to thaw it out. The wheat in the granary bin sounds like metallic pellets as you scoop up a bucketfull for the chickens. There is a little warmth inside the chicken coop, together with a heavy odor of ammonia and the flutter of a hen, startled into momentarily losing her perch on the roost. She regains her equilibrium, shakes her feathers, and half clucks in her sleep.

The milk cow is warm too, but many a winter morning I have wished her stone cold! Warm and massive, she munches contentedly at a scoopful of oats, turning her head from time to time to see what you are about, gazing at you with her soft eyes and breathing out mild clouds of vapor through her nostrils, as inoffensive a creature as you could imagine. But it is quite different at the end where you must work. She has prepared for your coming by lying all night in the deepest muck of the corral. You must scrape before you can brush, brush before you can sponge, sponge before you can wipe, and when you have finally cleaned it up the best you can, you hover anxiously over the milk bucket, trying to protect it from falling debris. But as you strip the last milk from the udder, she suddenly swings her tail, releasing an avalanche of filth. And so you carry the full bucket, not into the house, but to the pigpen, whose inhabitants, untroubled by fastidiousness, slurp and snort gleefully at the rich breakfast.

The success stories I read when I was a boy typically began with the ambitious young hero milking a dozen cows by lamplight each morning before trudging six miles through the snow to school. The stories did not tell how dirty a cow can get in an open corral in the winter, or how, no matter how many times you lather your hands with strong soap or how vigorously you scour your fingernails, you carry the smell of manure throughout the day. If success in life really depended on milking cows in one's youth, I would advise my sons to consider the advantages of failure.

Winter chores are one thing I am not sorry to have left behind. And yet in retrospect I can see that they are among the symbols of community life in the Mormon village. With the houses and barnyards clustered in town rather than scattered on the farms, we escaped much of the loneliness that I have since found recorded in many rural memoirs. Unpleasant tasks were made more bearable by the knowledge that others were doing the same thing at the same time. When I first stepped sleepily out of the house on those winter mornings, I might feel as cold and solitary as though I were the last survivor on a dying planet. But soon I would hear the familiar clatter of the weights on a neighbor's gate. Then the light would flare from the peak of their barn. A few minutes later, a third light would join our two, and then a fourth, and from down the block I would hear Billy Marshall singing to his cow. As light reached out to light, and sound to sound, a community was reborn. Though the distant stars still glittered coldly in a black sky above our islands of light, we knew that the night was over. The day had begun. We were the harbingers.

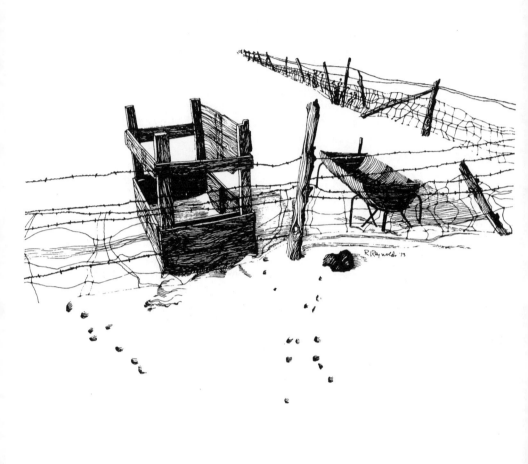

NINE

The Only Game in Town

A generation ago, community life in a southern Utah town tended to focus in a few places: the meetinghouse, the show house, the drugstore, and the pool hall. But during the winter months no place was more important than the high school gymnasium, where civic pride went on trial every Friday night. Basketball was the great game in rural Utah. There was scarcely a granary that did not have a hoop nailed to its side and a beaten patch of ground where the boys played after school, dribbling cautiously to avoid chicken droppings while they labored to perfect their "Arnie Ferrin" shot, a jump shot popularized by the star player on the University of Utah's 1947 NIT championship team.

A town's spirits rose and fell with the fortunes of the local high school team. The great hope was to gain the state tournament and get a crack at the big schools from upstate. Usually this moment of glory was very brief: a couple of lopsided games and quick elimination. But occasionally a rural school would make a run at the state championship. Our school's best showing, during my growing up years, came in 1948 when we won the fifth place consolation title. When the team came home, Walt Mortensen blew the fire whistle and we had a motorcade through town just as we had done on VJ Day.

In Poplarhaven, the gym was a tiny space with hardly enough room for the players, let alone spectators. If the floor had been much shorter, both teams could have shot free throws from the same line. Getting the ball out of backcourt was a cinch, since it took only three or four strides, but shooting layups required a special technique to avoid crashing into the wall behind the basket. Nevertheless, it was the scene of much glory, and my central childhood daydream involved charging down the floor to toss in the winning basket against the hated Bulldogs.

It was a dream not to be realized. The high point of my athletic career came when I was the sixth man on the seventh grade team, and

I never wore the varsity red and white even as a benchwarmer. Basketball remained as important to me as if I had been a star, however. I felt the same knot in my stomach on game day as did my friends who were on the team. I hurried through night chores, put on clean Levis, and walked downtown long before game time, my freshly slicked-down hair often freezing stiff in the cold air. I was usually among the first spectators to arrive, often getting there while the principal was still setting up the ticket table. I liked to be early so I could see the gym slowly come to life. The visiting team would arrive all in a group, having sometimes driven more than two hundred miles from Blanding or Monticello for the game. They kept close together, looking self-conscious and wary in alien country, wearing their letter jackets and carrying their gear in canvas bags. Our players arrived one by one, determinedly casual, confident of their superiority, brushing past the ticket-taker with scarcely a glance and striding across the floor toward the dressing room.

With them came the first of the crowd: Pep Club girls in red sweaters and skirts and white socks; other boys like myself, not good enough to make the team but never missing a game, hoping, by coming early, to get a chance to run the scoreboard or sweep the floor; farmers still in their chore clothes; brothers, sisters, parents, grandparents, even great-grandparents of the players. Soon the school block was lined with parked cars, and still the people came until it seemed as though the entire town were crammed into the tiny gym.

The crowd came early because one of the best parts of the evening was watching the team run onto the floor for warmups. The girls' dressing room, which was used by the visiting team, was accessible by a flight of stairs that opened directly onto the playing floor. To reach the home team dressing room, however, you first had to climb up onto the stage then go through a doorway and downstairs to the basement. This meant that while the visitors could only run onto the floor in an ordinary manner, our team could leap down impressively from the stage. It was a great moment when the team came charging off the stage, driving the basketball hard against the floor while the gym rang with the strains of the pep song, "We are the Rangers, riding along. . . ." Other teams might have played better basketball, but nobody ever beat our boys at jumping off a stage.

In my earliest memories, the scoreboard was a homemade device with slots in it. When a basket was made, the boys who ran the scoreboard had to fumble through a pile of numbered cards until they found the right numbers to insert into the slots. This was replaced by an electric scoreboard which showed the time as well as the score, but which used to break down with remarkable regularity. There was never anything wrong with it that could be discovered before the game, but it seemed that invariably, at the moment of highest tension, something would go haywire. Then play would cease while Osmer Johnson, the town electrician, climbed down from the bleachers to take a look. After studying the situation for a while, he would pull a screwdriver out of his pocket and poke tentatively at a connection or two. He knew, as we all did, that the scoreboard would come on again in its own good time, and it always did.

Every high school has one traditional rival whose games mean more than any others. For us it was South Emery, the school from the other end of the county. A casual observer driving through the string of villages nestled against the mountains might not have been able to recognize the dividing line between the two schools, but we had no doubt that the civilization at our end of the county was of a higher order than that at the other end. Every contest was a war with the barbarians, right against wrong.

You would have thought that the gym was full to capacity for other games, but we always managed to pack twice as many people in when we played South Emery. Their gym was, if anything, a little smaller than ours, but it made no difference. It was as though on a certain Friday night each winter, the whole county tilted to the south and the population flowed down to the gym in Ferron. Then, a month or so later, it tilted the other way and the whole population flowed to Poplarhaven. The homemade plank bleachers were jammed. People stood in the doorways and against the walls, and crowded even onto the playing floor itself. Those who couldn't squeeze into the gym jammed the hall outside and got reports on the progress of the game from the luckier ones who could see. The noise, of course, was deafening. Each school had a few special cheers that were reserved for this game, and as insults passed from one side of the hall to the other emotions rose higher and higher. Once a section of bleachers collapsed under the South Emery Pep Club, and I felt a surge of exultation, since they were winning the game at the time, before it occurred to me that somebody might be hurt. Such contests can work a wonderful simplification of moral complexities.

But these feelings, for all their intensity, were strangely evanescent. When the final buzzer had sounded, and each team had given the other the obligatory rah-rah, the crowd, still hot and noisy, was herded out into the hallway so they could be charged another admission for the dance. While the orchestra set up their traps in a corner, Jewell Rowley, the janitor, flung open the high windows to release the overheated air and made a few passes up and down the floor scattering soap flakes from a box he carried under his arm. Then the lights were turned down, the music began, and soon the bitterest rivals were drifting around the floor in each other's arms, red and white and blue and white together.

Between dances there were a few spontaneous yells, "North beat South!" or "South beat North!" And there might be a fist fight or two outside on the lawn before the night was over, but more likely for personal than patriotic reasons. Like the shield of Achilles, the cracker-box gym was large enough to encompass a world at peace as well as a world at war, to be a ceremonial dancing ground for the graceful young as well as the arena in which, again next year, the superiority of this or that end of the county would have to be proved in a trial by combat.

TEN

Spring

I understand that in the rural districts of Ireland the first day of February is regarded as the beginning of spring. On that day, no matter if the weather is good or bad, a bit of ground is symbolically plowed and an inventory taken of the fodder to see if there is enough to last until harvest. In Utah, too, you might say that spring begins on the first of February. Or you might choose the first of April, or the first of June. Each of those days is about equally likely to be springlike, and equally likely to be followed by a snowstorm the day after. Spring in Utah is not so much a season as it is a handful of pleasant days scattered through the last half of a six-month winter. "Springtime in the Rockies" may be the best known song to come out of the state, but it wisely avoids saying much about the climate, preferring to dwell upon the blue eyes of the little sweetheart of the mountains, which, unlike the sky, are constant in their color.

The one thing you can really depend on in a Utah spring is mud. And no mud could be muddier than Poplarhaven mud. Indeed, our valley may be the only place where you can wade in the mud and have dust blow in your face at the same time. No matter how dry the winter, there was always mud in the spring, not just an occasional puddle but mud that went deep, deep. Main Street was paved, and there were a couple of gravelled side streets, but the other roads were an adventure in travel, slippery here, deeply rutted there, and in the low places bottomless. The town fathers tried to improve the situation by building up the roads with rock—not crushed gravel, but rock just as it came from the hills, with boulders as big as footballs. They dumped truckloads of this stuff into the swampy places, and for several months the cars would lurch and buck over the bumpy roadbed. Then the rock would gradually sink into the mud, and they would have to haul in more loads to keep people from getting stuck.

Not only was the mud deep, it was also sticky, a paste-like blue clay that clung to everything it touched. You couldn't ride a bicycle for half a block before the fenders were so badly clogged that the wheels could not turn. When I walked home from school, the mud accumulated on my shoes until I could hardly lift my feet. Mother used to watch for me from the kitchen window, and when I came into sight she would run to the door and shout, "Don't come in the house! Don't come in the house!"

Spring wasn't all bad. If it brought a raw wind that cut through our clothes and chapped our hands, it also brought clear, sparkling days such as I have never seen anywhere except in our valley. Often the difference between winter and spring was just a bit of shelter. No matter how cold the air, there was warmth in the bricks on the south wall of Maurice Jensen's store, where the first dandelions bloomed each year, their round, yellow heads turned in full faith toward the sun. And there were some genuinely warm days, sometimes two or three weeks at a stretch, long enough for the apricot buds to swell. Then, when the blossoms hung heavy and fragrant on the trees, spring would play its usual trick. An ominous wind would start up in the afternoon, though the sun still shone brightly, and we would wake up the next morning to six inches of snow.

But spring is not so much a state of the weather as it is a state of the mind. And so we never wore our winter coats after the first of March. We laid out our gardens and planted our peas in the clammy soil. We put fresh sawdust in the high jump pit at school and marked fresh lanes on the running track to prepare for the county track meet, always held on a windy day that whipped the dust across the square but a great occasion nonetheless. And no matter how bad the weather we went Eastering.

Easter was the great spring ritual, but it was hardly a religious holiday. Indeed, regular church-attenders were likely to be absent on Easter Sunday because they were out in the desert, part of a great unorganized exodus from the towns. For families it was usually a single day's outing and picnic, but for the teenagers it was much more. I don't know exactly how far back the tradition of Eastering in the desert went, but my father used to tell of going out with his friends in a wagon, camping in Bull Hollow or Buckhorn Draw, and getting into fights with the boys from Cleveland. For my mother as a girl it was always Easter at The Breaks. I looked forward eagerly to the time when I would be old enough to sluff school for several days and go far, far out in the desert, clear to the Sindbad country. I can remember watching with envy, when I was in the sixth or seventh grade, as a gang of high school boys left town on Wednesday afternoon in Bud Nielson's Army surplus truck with no visible supplies except for several cases of soda pop. That year my friends and I hiked down to Lone Island for the day, roasted wieners over a sagebrush fire, clambered through washes and caves formed in the soft clay, and were smoking cedar bark cigars when Lund Leonard arrived to see if we wanted a ride home.

The time eventually came when we could go Eastering as the older boys had done. We made a three- or four-day excursion of it, lived on Twinkies and soda pop, climbed the slick rock of The Wedge, tossed rocks into the San Rafael River from the suspended bridge, and tried to scale Windowblind Castle. It was the very opposite of a wilderness experience, as there were always other parties nearby, the desert being more populous than the towns at Eastertime. We spent much of the day looking for shelter from the wind, and at night we huddled in our bedrolls wishing we were back home. The whole thing was a sort of nature ritual, like a rain dance which is performed not because there is rain but because there is not. We acted as if it were spring in hopes of making the season a reality.

The Easter I remember best is the first one I can recall in any detail. I couldn't have been more than four or five years old at the time. We didn't go down to the desert that year but up into the foothills with Uncle Theo and his family. I had spent the day before in boiling and coloring Easter eggs. Young as I was, I had picked up an image of rolling colored eggs down a gentle, grassy slope, and I was disappointed, when we reached our destination, to find nothing but dry bunchgrass and stunted sage and Brigham tea. While Mother spread a blanket in the shelter of a big rock and laid out the picnic supplies, I picked out my hill and labored to the top, clutching my Easter basket. There was still no green grass to be seen, but a slope I undeniably had before me, and I selected my best egg to roll. I can still see that egg tumbling down the rocky hillside with bits of blue shell and white and yellow flesh flying off this way and that. Standing there in the brilliant April sunshine and the cold April wind, watching my Easter egg disintegrate, I think I got my first inkling that life was going to be much more complicated than I had imagined.

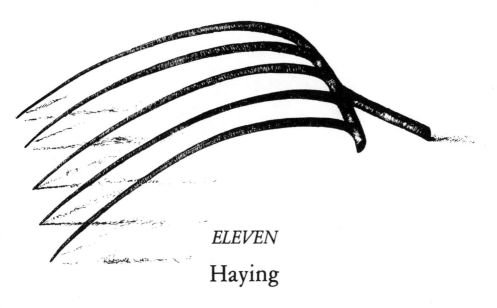

ELEVEN

Haying

"The fact is the sweetest dream that labor knows."
—Robert Frost, "Mowing"

I don't know what the meadowlarks say anywhere else, but in our valley, when I was a boy, they used to say, "Utah's a pretty little place." Summer mornings always began with the meadowlark's song. One bird quite close by, perhaps on the pasture fence, would put forth his claim, the first syllables lengthened out, the rest of the phrase enunciated rapidly: "U-u-u-t-a-a-h-'s aprettylittleplace." This was sometimes varied with just the "Utah" syllables, as if the bird were trying to think of some other observation to make. But he could never find anything more appropriate, and he always concluded in the same way: "Utah . . . Utah . . . Utah's a pretty little place." Then an answer would come from another meadowlark up the road by the mill, not contradicting but reaffirming, "Utah's a pretty little place."

I saw no reason to doubt the meadowlark's claim. Our valley might not have seemed pretty to everyone, but I thought it was the loveliest place on earth, and summer was the loveliest time, especially early summer. The gray, barren hills made the green fields seem all the richer by contrast, and at daybreak the sky was almost always cloudless, the mountain air incredibly sweet. As the day progressed, the morning's enchantment could be dulled somewhat by the heat and dust and the weeds awaiting the hoe in the vegetable garden. But these were only passing shadows. There would still be time for swimming in the creek or tubing in the canal, for hikes to the hideout in the foothills or horseback rides up the canyon. And there would be day after day like this, as changeless as the meadowlark's song.

Thus the leisurely days of early summer ran on until one morning when the clatter of the mowing machine came through the window as a rhythmic background to the meadowlark's refrain, and I caught the first sweet whiff of crushed alfalfa and knew that Grandpa had begun cutting the hay.

As a young child, before I had to work in the hay, I used to hurry through breakfast and run out to the field to watch Grandpa. In those days, agricultural technology had changed little since the 1890s, when horse-drawn mowing machines and dump rakes and Jackson forks first came to the valleys of southern Utah. The fields, small themselves, were broken into smaller patches of two or three acres, rotated among diversified crops of hay and grain. Grandpa cut one patch at a time, riding the mowing machine behind Old Belle and Prince, leaning a little to the right on the spring seat to watch for clogs while the cutting arm ran noisily but invisibly along the ground, its progress revealed by the sudden collapse of the standing alfalfa into a level swath. At the end of the run Grandpa would rein in the team, push a lever to raise the cutting arm off the ground, and bring the horses around to a new heading: "Whoa, back! Gee, now! Gee, Belle, gee! Back, back! Giddy-up!" And the arm would drop again into the hay, the horses strain forward, the clatter resume.

The mowing machine fascinated me, and frightened me as well because I had been filled with stories from Mother and Grandma of children who had had their legs cut off while playing in the hay. The rapidly oscillating knife could do that, I knew, as easily as it clipped off the alfalfa stems, as easily as it sliced through the bodies of unfortunate pheasants who waited an instant too long before trying to fly. Grandpa sometimes had me hold up the end of the mower knife while he honed the teeth at the grindstone in the dooryard. Perched on a bicycle-like frame, he made the stone go around by pedaling with his feet, while a tin can suspended above the stone slowly dripped water to lubricate it and make it grind finer. The wicked-looking triangular teeth shone brightly, and Grandpa paused in his pedaling from time to time to test an edge with a cautious thumb while I stood as still as I could, arms aching from having to hold the knife just so while the water went drip, drip, drip, and the bees buzzed lazily among the hollyhocks.

Putting up hay demands precise timing, as the crop must dry rapidly to just the right degree for the highest quality. Too dry, and valuable leaves are lost in the handling; too wet, and the hay will spoil. One day in the Utah sun could dry the cut alfalfa sufficiently for the next stage of windrowing. So the second day of haying season began with the creak, creak of the dump rake as an accompaniment to the meadowlark's song, and in place of the rich perfume of new-mown hay there was a crisp, tonic aroma in the air. The mechanical operations of mowing and raking Grandpa always did himself, as though no one else could be trusted to get the rows straight or avoid breaking the mower knife on a rock. But as soon as the hay was in windrows, there was plenty of work for everyone, and the idle days of early summer were only a memory.

Nothing looks nicer than a field of haycocks ready for hauling, but no farming task is more tedious than piling hay—except, perhaps, for shocking grain, an equally picturesque and equally boring operation. Piling is not heavy work, but it is hot and itchy work and seemingly unproductive since the hay still remains in the field when you are finished, as though nothing had really been accomplished. There are no natural breaks in the labor, as there are in hauling hay, and nothing to look forward to but the end of the patch. I remember the hours of going up and down the windrows, shaping the piles and gathering up any wisps the rake had missed, for Grandpa would not tolerate waste. Uncle Merlin was the best hay piler, moving briskly along with a steady rhythm of thrust, turn, gather, thrust, turn, gather. I sometimes tried to imitate his motions and would advance vigorously for a dozen piles or so. But the field stretched on and on; I soon lost my energy and returned to a plodding pace, relying on various devices to mark the passing of time: another fifty piles and I could take a short break to go to the ditch and plunge my head into the water, washing away the sweat and leaving my hair wet and cool under my straw hat; another twenty windrows and we would be almost half done.

While we piled the hay, Grandpa would be cutting another

patch, to be raked the next morning in advance of the pilers. This continued patch by patch through the home field, first field, and farther field until the entire crop stood ranged in neat piles, a pleasant sight to behold when it was done, though insufficient reward for the labor required to produce it.

Hauling hay was a much more sociable job than piling and more satisfying in every way. There were usually four or five men and boys working together as a team: pitchers on each side of the hayrack to throw on the piles of hay and a tromper to build the load. If there weren't enough family members available to make up a crew, Grandma would call around to find a hired man. In Poplarhaven, as in most rural areas, there was a contingent of landless men who held no regular employment but picked up a narrow income by hiring out as field hands during the harvest season and doing odd jobs the rest of the year. The first hired man I can remember was Silas Cox, who died when I was very young. Later there was Wallace Knight, a kind and pious man but a very slow worker. I can recall watching him load manure on one occasion when he carefully set out a spare pitchfork in case the handle of the first fork should grow too hot from friction. Even at that early age, I sensed that a pitchfork in his hands would never overheat. After Wallace Knight was drafted into the Army, the hired man was usually either Len Wight, who was deaf and loved to tease, or Jack Horrocks, a bear-like man with great strength and a morose disposition who muttered a continuous stream of vague complaints and threats as he worked. We rarely had more than one hired man at a time on the hay crew. Since haying was a busy season throughout the community, there was considerable competition for the available hands. Moreover, the men were suspicious and resentful of one another, each feeling that the others were not doing their share of the work.

The day's crew assembled early in Grandpa's barnyard, or at any rate it always seemed early to me, though Grandpa had already put in several hours of work by the time the rest of us arrived. Belle and Prince were hitched to the hayrack, a wide wooden platform attached to wagon running gear, with a six-foot ladder attached at the front to provide access to the load. We all sat on the edges of the hayrack for the trip to the field, all except Grandpa, who stood beside the ladder holding the reins in his hands. The hayrack had no springs, and the iron-tired wheels jolted mercilessly across the ruts and furrows, but if you gripped the edge of the rack with both hands, to absorb some of the shock, and arched your spine to absorb some more, the trip was tolerable.

There is a science to building a load of hay. The corners must be established first and kept slightly ahead of the middle or else the load will taper off too soon. But if the corners get too far ahead, they are apt to slide off. The load must be constructed in order, each forkful of hay tied to the others to form a single, relatively stable unit. With properly cured alfalfa it is easy to build a good load. Clover, with its coarse stems, is harder to work with, and grass hay is hardest of all since the stems are slippery and will not cling together. The most carefully constructed load of grass hay is liable to slide off the wagon the first time you cross a ditch.

There is a hierarchy as well as cooperation among a hay crew, with pitchers having the highest status. A good pitcher is a model of grace and rhythm as he strides alongside the moving hayrack, thrusting his pitchfork into each pile and levering it onto the load in one smooth arc. But someone must tromp, and the lot usually falls to the lowest ranking member of the crew. Tromping is miserable work as you must move about on the unsteady load, your legs sinking into the hay at every step, while you try to pack each forkful firmly into place. The dust and chaff stick to your skin and fill your nostrils, and if the field happens to be weedy there will inevitably be foxtail stems that get inside your trouser legs and work their way upward, tormenting you with their prickling.

The beginner in the hayfield starts out as an assistant tromper, floundering around and trying to keep out of the way while having to endure, moreover, the teasing comments of the pitchers about boys who failed to keep on top of the load and were later found buried in the hay. After this initiation, you might be promoted, if that is the word, to tromper, with full responsibility for the shape of the load, full blame if there is a weak corner or if Grandpa can't get as much on the wagon as he had hoped. At fifteen or sixteen, if you had grown tall enough, you might hope to move up to pitcher, but there was nothing certain about this promotion since it depended on the availability of somebody else to tromp. I learned that it was best not to say anything but simply to jump off the hayrack and begin pitching piles on before the others got started. Then the hired man, a little slow on the uptake, might fall into the role of tromper by default, though he would cast resentful glances and occasional slighting remarks in my direction as we loaded the hay.

We used to say, with considerable pride, that Grandpa hauled haystacks instead of loads. The horses pulled the hayrack slowly up and down the rows, guided by voice commands except at the end of the patch, where Grandpa would grasp Old Belle's bridle to lead them around and start them up the next row. The load grew steadily until it was above the ladder, but that was far from the end. When the pitchers could no longer reach to place their piles on the load, they would use their pitchforks as catapults to fling the hay up to be caught by the tromper and put into place. Finally, when we could scarcely throw the forkfuls higher, Grandpa would pause, lean on his pitchfork, take off his hat, wipe his bald head with his handkerchief, and announce, "Well, that's about a load."

Then came the ascent of the green mountain. The tromper would plant his pitchfork in the hay to provide a handhold above the ladder. One by one the pitchers would climb to the top of the ladder, then reach for the fork handle, and finally grasp the tromper's hand and scramble to the summit, where each one made himself a nest, not too close to the edge, and settled down for the trip to the haystack. Grandpa always came last, untying the reins from the ladder and carrying them over his arm as he climbed. Several yards of well cured hay make an excellent cushion, so there was none of the tooth-rattling jolting of the journey out but instead a soft rocking motion as if we were sailing on a gentle sea. We could not relax too much, though, for at least once in every season the load would slide off in a ditch as we crossed, dumping hay, men, and pitchforks in one confused heap. It seemed, too, as if there had to be the annual runaway. Belle and Prince were not a skittish team by any means, but you could never tell when the unexpected eruption of a pheasant or the sight of a rag fluttering on a fence might send them into sudden panic. Those on the wagon, if they were wise, would slide off at once rather than trying to ride it out, and the team would knock down gates and shatter the planks of the hayrack and tear their harnesses before they finally ran themselves out. Then they would stand exhausted in the road, their muzzles foam-flecked, their legs trembling as they awaited Grandpa's wrath.

The hay from the home field was stored in the barn, but most of the crop from the other fields was stacked beside the straw-thatched shed in the first field. The dry climate allows exposed haystacks, and the rural West is still littered with the derricks that were once used to stack the hay. More than forty different hay derrick designs have been catalogued, some of them ingenious contraptions that could pivot as well as lift. We used the very simplest kind of derrick, merely a long pole planted in the ground at an angle so that it leaned out over the stack and was supported by guy wires to keep it steady. (Jack Horrocks managed to knock down a guy post at least once a year as he backed his old Plymouth out of the shed. He always came back on his own time with a shovel to set a new post, but he muttered with special bitterness as he did it, as though this were further evidence of a grand conspiracy against his peace of mind.) A steel cable ran through a pulley at the top of the haypole to another pulley at its base, where Old Belle was hitched to the cable. By this means we lifted the forkfuls of hay from the wagon to where they could swing out over the stack and be released on the desired spot.

The hayforks were manufactured items and showed less variety than the homemade derricks. I can remember only three types. The harpoon fork was shaped like an inverted U with prongs that could be driven into the hay and toggles that were turned to hold the hay on the fork. The grappler fork had two sets of steel prongs that could be closed like jaws to seize a giant mouthful of hay. But we always used the Jackson fork, four long curving tines on a rigid triangular frame that pivoted from a steel yoke attached to the cable. The tines were driven into the hay and the yoke latched to the frame. At the signal, the cable horse would lift the forkful out of the load. When the fork reached the right place, Grandpa pulled the triprope, releasing the latch and allowing the hay to fall. While many of our neighbors swore by the harpoon or the grappler, we had no doubt about the superiority of the Jackson fork, which could lift as much as a tenth of a load at a bite.

At the barn, the fork ran on a trolley along a track at the roof ridge. The roof extended out from the front of the barn so that the hayrack could be pulled under it. The cable horse worked at the rear of the barn, out of sight of the load, so a relay system was necessary for commands. Grandpa would drive the fork into the load, throwing his weight against it to get as big a bite as possible, then stand back with the triprope held loosely in his hand and shout, "All right!" "Awright!" would be the command relayed by the stackers inside the barn, and the boy on the cable horse would urge her into motion. Old Belle would strain at first as the cable grew taut and the forkful slowly separated from the load and rose on its pulleys toward the track. When it hit the trolley it latched and began to roll easily along the track until it reached the right place in the barn. Then the stackers shouted, "Yo!" and Grandpa tugged the rope, tripping the fork and allowing the hay to fall in a cloud of choking dust. Feeling the tug, the boy on Old Belle would turn her around, dig his heels into her broad sides, and try to urge her to a trot while the cable snaked slowly back through the pulleys as Grandpa pulled the rope. When the trolley reached the end of the track, the fork dropped to the hayrack, making the cable shriek and slap the back of the barn and kick up a dust cloud under Old Belle's hooves.

As a young child, I was torn between the appeal of riding the cable horse with my cousin Ted and that of helping Grandpa pull the fork out of the barn. Sometimes he let me pull it by myself, and I would strain with all my might, trying to accelerate at the end so the trolley would latch properly and release the fork. Then I turned around quickly to watch it fall onto the hayrack, marvelling how Grandpa was able to keep from being impaled on the vicious tines.

At eight or nine, I took Ted's place on the cable horse, and he became a stacker inside the barn. A few years later, I became a stacker myself. Stacking is exhausting labor, as you must work in stifling heat and in air that is almost unbreathable. When the fork drops its load, you have to work feverishly to move the hay to the sides of the barn before the next forkful comes in. At the end of a load, you emerge flushed and dripping, with dark perspiration stains on your shirt and hay leaves plastered to your skin.

After unloading there was always a short break for a drink of water from the hydrant, if we were at the barn, or if we were unloading at the shed we would pass around the dripping water bag and gulp down the cool, canvas-tasting fluid. Sometimes Uncle Merlin brought a gallon jar of lemonade wrapped in a wet towel, an exquisite refreshment for a throat raw with hay dust. Then it was back to the field for another load.

The noontime load always went to the barn. When we had finished unloading it, Grandpa would feed and water the horses while the rest of us rolled up our sleeves and lathered our arms and necks and faces with the bar of soap placed by the hydrant on the lawn. Then we trooped into the house for the dinner that Grandma had prepared. Dinner represented a significant portion of the day's pay for the hired men, who took advantage of it by putting away great quantities of fried meat and mashed potatoes and gravy and warm biscuits and honey. Jack Horrocks ate in the same manner as he worked, with a glum intensity, but Len Wight glowed with pleasure at the table, grinning wider as each new dish was passed and gabbling volubly between mouthfuls in his almost incomprehensible nasal tones. After the meal, we lay on the shady lawn for twenty minutes or so, until Grandpa judged that the horses had had enough rest. Then it was back to the field for an afternoon shift that could last for six or seven hours, until the sun dropped to the rim of the high plateau.

I remember haying season as very long, but in fact it occupied only three weeks or so, from late June to mid-July, for the first cutting, and another three weeks in August for the second crop. Still, it was the major harvest, the central activity of summer. And it was more: more than the hot, dusty labor, more than the wide stubble fields, more than the sensation of relief when you could lower your weary limbs into the bathtub at day's end. It was the immemorial gathering, the celebration of human dependence on the good earth. That was the real basis for the fellowship of the hay crew, for the stories retold, on long trips to the barn, of past harvests, memorable tip-overs and famous runaways, eccentric farmhands of earlier generations. Nor was it merely a private celebration, for it involved the entire community. The narrow lanes were filled with hayracks going back and forth from town to field, from field to town, and we rarely completed a trip without having to pull way over into the barrow pit to allow another wagon to pass while we exchanged friendly insults with the crew, and perhaps fought a brief skirmish with green apples that we had stuffed inside our shirts. The very landscape seemed to join in the spirit of the harvest. The cottonwood trees along the farm lanes and the gateposts in town wore fragrant garlands gleaned from passing loads, as though they too were celebrating. With the groaning of the laden wagons, the creaking of the derricks, the neighing of the teams, the shouts of the stackers, it was as if everything, animate or inanimate, were somehow joining in the chorus of the meadowlark's song, a symphony of joy and praise for the beauty of the place.

TWELVE

Three Cheers

Utahns have two patriotic holidays in July instead of just one. On the Fourth we celebrate Independence Day along with the rest of the country, and the Twenty-fourth is Pioneer Day, commemorating the arrival of the first company of Mormon pioneers in the Salt Lake Valley in 1847. As a child I knew that the Fourth and the Twenty-fourth were both important days, but it took me a long time to get their significance straight, to get firmly fixed in my mind which was the state holiday and which the national. My confusion probably arose in part from the fact that the two dates both had fours in them and came so close together. But I think, too, that there was a general tendency in our town to merge the themes of the holidays, to make both of them celebrations of all our patriotic sentiments, local, state, and national.

The same images cling to both dates in my memory—band music, ball games, sparklers, firecrackers, hot dogs, potato chips— but they cling more closely to the Twenty-fourth than to the Fourth. The greater emphasis on the Twenty-fourth did not reflect a hierarchy of loyalties so much as it did certain practical considerations. The Fourth of July came in the middle of haying, while the Twenty-fourth fell during the interval between the first and second cuttings when we had more time to celebrate. In addition, since the Twenty-fourth was connected with the church, the various ward organizations, Relief Society, Mutual, Primary, Sunday School, were available to take charge of different parts of the festivities. So while the American Legion and the Lions Club usually worked up something for the Fourth, the Twenty-fourth was our grand community celebration.

Preparations started well in advance of the big day, beginning with band practices. Along about the first of the month, Mr. Peterson would gather up the available members of the high school band for two or three evening practices each week. Band practice gave us an excuse to get away from the hay field at a reasonable hour, so we welcomed these sessions, especially when we were younger and not yet full-fledged band members. Because some members of the senior band were unavailable in the summertime, we were allowed to practice and perform with the older kids, which made us feel very important. We marched and played for an hour or two in the falling dusk and then, when practice was over, spent the rest of the evening wandering up and down Main Street or sprawled on the school lawn listening to the high school boys brag. I recall one memorable night in my fifteenth summer when several of us walked out to Black's Hill after band practice with a comparable number of older girls. We sat on the rocky slope for an hour or so watching the lights come on while the girls told spicy jokes and taught us how to kiss. Then we walked arm in arm back into town, with boys and girls gradually peeling off from the group as we walked up Center Street until only Jerrold Cook and I were left, still dazed with pleasure, to compare notes on the experience as we walked home.

The Twenty-fourth of July began at dawn with the firing of the "cannon," actually two or three sticks of dynamite exploded one after another in the square, which rattled windows and jarred people out of sleep throughout the town. Then the band members had to hurry down to the high school, where we piled onto a hayrack and went up and down the streets playing martial airs to the awakening town, to children sitting on front porches in their pajamas and old women out in their gardens gathering the produce before the sun shone on it. After the band serenade, there was a break of a couple of hours while morning chores were done. Then at nine o'clock everyone gathered on Main Street for the parade.

The parade was much the same every year. Indeed, I have a photograph taken at the turn of the century which shows the Twenty-fourth of July parade forming by the park, and everything looks remarkably familiar in it. It is essentially the same parade that I watched forty or fifty years later. Main Street in Poplarhaven is immensely wide, so there was plenty of room for spectators to park their cars along the street, backing in to the curb (if there had been any curb) so that the seats faced the street. The adults watched from the cars where they could be comfortable and honk appreciatively at each entry, while the children climbed onto the fenders for a closer view. The parade was led by the marshall of the day, who was always dressed and whiskered as Brigham Young. Depending on "Brig-

ham's" age and agility, he would either ride on horseback or in a
buckboard, waving and nodding to the crowd with great dignity.
Behind Brigham came the band and then the floats, perhaps twenty
in number. Two or three would be rather elaborate productions, with
log cabins or exploring parties or Indian battles in full array on a hayrack. Other wagons would be more simply garnished with sagebrush,
and several of the floats were merely cars with a few strands of crepe
paper strung on them. Some floats—fewer each year—carried
pioneers, and others the several "queens" and their attendants—
Miss Liberty, Miss Deseret, Miss Utah, Miss Castle Valley 1877, Miss
Castle Valley 1949, and so on, enough symbolic misses to include a
good portion of the teenaged girls in town. And there was the perennial Primary float, a hayrack packed with young children and bearing
a butcher paper banner proclaiming "Utah's Best Crop." Behind the
floats came two dozen boys on horseback and bicycle, shirtless and
painted as Indians, whooping and yelling as they rode. The parade
slowly moved up Main Street for four blocks to Jack Corgiat's garage
then turned around and came back down again, making it twice as
long and allowing the spectators to see both sides of the floats.

After the parade, we went to the meetinghouse for the program.
Here, under the direction of "Brigham Young," a series of songs and
tap dances and readings and trombone solos unfolded that was as pre-
dictable and yet as much enjoyed as the parade. Each number was
met not only by applause but by first one man and then another—
Heber Leonard, Pierce Wilson, Frank Robbins—rising to his feet in
the audience and shouting, "Three cheers for these here little gals!"
or "Three cheers for Miss Poplarhaven!" Then we all joined in, some
of us rather self-consciously, not with the staccato cheers that you hear
in movies, but slowly, giving each syllable its full value while the
leader set the tempo by waving his arm in circles above his head:
"H-i-i-p, h-i-i-p, hooray! H-i-i-p, h-i-i-p, hooray! H-i-i-p, h-i-i-p,
hooray!" The last item on the program was Brigham Young's ora-
tion, which like most other parts of the celebration mingled the occasions of the Fourth and the Twenty-fourth. He would remind us that
we should be proud to be Americans, and Utahns, and Mormons,
and citizens of Poplarhaven, and declared that a great destiny awaited
us in these valleys of the mountains. The speech would be interrupted from time to time by cheers: "Three cheers for the Constitu-
tion!" "Three cheers for the pioneers!" And at the end, those with

yet unexpended acclaim would jump to their feet and try to out-yell one another: "Three cheers for Brigham Young!" "Three cheers for the United States of America!" "Three cheers for the parade committee!"

The afternoon began with races and games in the park for the children, followed by a baseball game between the town team—a pick-up crew made up of young and middle-aged men who had no regular uniforms and carried all their equipment in a couple of gunnysacks—and a usually better-equipped team from Hiawatha or one of the other coal camps. They played on the dusty square, with young boys shagging foul balls from the irrigation ditches. Through it all we gorged ourselves on greasy hamburgers and hot dogs dispensed from makeshift booths by men with red faces and white aprons, and on bottled soda pop fished out of ice-filled washtubs.

By the time the ball game was over, we were usually tired and a little queasy, ready for a return to normality in the form of evening chores. But the Twenty-fourth was not yet concluded. There was still the open-air dance to be held on the tennis court. Outdoor dances were a tradition from the glory days of the Wilberg resort which had drawn young people from all across the valley in my parents' generation. I thought it must be the height of romance to dance under the stars with a lovely girl in your arms while the canyon breeze blew cool across the dark valley. By the time I grew old enough to attend, though, the summer dances were on the decline and most of the magic was gone. Or perhaps it was simply that the actuality never measures up to the expectation and that in my daydreams I had not anticipated how awkward I would be when I got on the dance floor with a flesh-and-blood girl and discovered in horror that I had nothing to say to her.

Whatever the reason, the dances I remember most fondly are not those I legitimately attended but those of my childhood, when I might steal back downtown and lie on the trodden grass of the park to watch and listen. The impression was strong enough that, even today, when I see an isolated tennis court I am likely to think not of tennis but of dancing, and to hear in my imagination the wailing of Orson Peterson's saxophone and the rich chords of Ora Larsen at the piano and the plinking of Dad's banjo. The tunes that still echo in my memory come from the great era of American popular song and evoke for most listeners an air of sophistication, the ambience of Broadway or Harlem in the 1930s. But for me they are undissolubly linked to summer nights in a wide, bare Utah valley, where their haunting strains helped to transform the commonplace into the memorable and made a fitting climax to a celebration that was the high point of the village year.

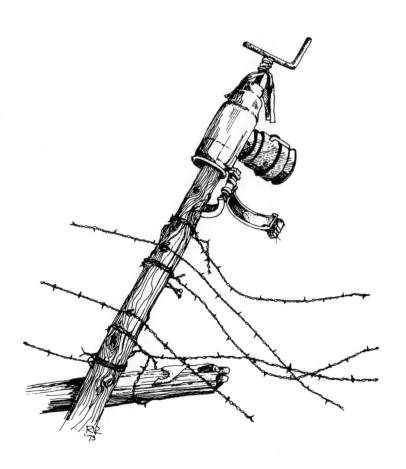

THIRTEEN

Going Back to School

When we stepped out into the freedom of the May sunshine on the final half-day, we preferred not to think that we would ever enter the schoolhouse again. But three and a half months of weeds and hay leaves worked a change, and so, when the summer heat broke at the end of August and we awoke one morning to a different taste in the air, a different smell to the earth, it was natural to think about going back to school.

Opening day was one of our rituals. It started with an ear-reddening scrubbing on Sunday night, even though there had been the Saturday bath just the night before. Then on Monday morning you put on for the first time the new clothes that had come in the mail from Gumpy Wards, the shoes too tight, the pants stiff, and the bright print shirt crisp to the touch and smelling of dye. After the invariable breakfast of bacon and hard fried eggs and germade swimming in yellow cream, you set out for the mile-long walk to school, becoming, as you drew nearer the center of town, part of a great convergence, other kids similarly tentative in their new clothes after a season of bare feet and ragged knees, girls with tight braids, high school boys superior in their never-to-be-laundered white corduroys. Inside the schoolhouse the smell of fresh varnish rose from the shiny floorboards, and the alphabet marched in alternating upper and lower case across the front of the classroom above the clean blackboard. After you found your place in the old-fashioned files where the front of your desk was somebody else's seat—usually somebody whose pigtails hung temptingly within reach—you made a preliminary survey of the initials and dates carved by the previous occupants, a sort of informal history of the school to which, later on (but certainly not on the first day!), you might add another chapter.

There is nothing like the first day of school to give you the sense of a fresh start, with the mistakes of the past all forgotten and a future as flawless and bright with promise as your new yellow pencil and your fresh box of crayons and the UISSCO notebook with the beehive on its brown marbled cover and all those clean lined pages inside. For the first morning, at least, going back to school is paradise regained.

So I remember it, at any rate. But not long ago I ran across the report of a speech given by a state school official in which he warned that students in small rural schools "are being deprived of educational opportunities that could be most meaningful and useful in their lives." That statement puzzled me at first. My own educational deprivation in a small-town school must have been so severe that it deprived me even of the sense of being deprived. On further reflection, however, I have managed to gain at least a partial awareness of the inadequacy of my early education.

The grade school in Poplarhaven was an old, high-ceilinged, echoing building with big, bare rooms: certainly not what you would call a stimulating learning environment. And it had windows, which are a terrible distraction, a whole wall of tall windows in every classroom through which we could see the trees and mountains and clouds. If you were to add up the time I spent gazing out of the windows and daydreaming, it would probably come to at least two or three years of lost educational opportunities that could have been most meaningful and useful in my life. We were also deprived of organized recreational activities. Our playground was the bare earth of the town square, and we had, if I remember correctly, a single soccer ball and a softball and bat for our equipment. Still, necessity is the mother of invention, and we managed to get through recesses and noon hour pretty well, with marbles and jacks and hopscotch. The school was surrounded by a low fence of steel pipe, which was terribly inadequate by modern standards as we could easily go over or under it and get out into the street, which we regularly did in order to run across to Maurice Jensen's or the Oleander to buy penny candy. The pipes were at just the right level, however, for the girls to use them as tricky bars, and this supplied amusement for the boys as well, since we would watch them as they twirled in hopes of catching a glimpse of their underwear. In the winter we built snow forts and engaged in pitched battles at recess or marked out pathways in the snow for games of fox and geese. When spring came, we chased the dust devils that whipped across the square, thinking it great fun to get into the middle of the whirlwind and feel the particles of dirt pelting our faces and hair. And then we could usually count on a schoolyard fight every day or two that we could enjoy until some do-gooder girl ran for the principal and he came out brandishing the "board of education" and hauled the combatants off to his office to contemplate their offenses.

Now that I come to think of them, our deprivations were almost too numerous to list. We had no media center or media specialists, no remediation experts, no counselors or school psychologists, no teachers' aides, no special education, no enrichment. We didn't even have a proper library, just a big closet next to the sixth grade room where old textbooks were stored. Once a week the closet was opened, and we could choose books from it to read. Not a very satisfactory arrangement, certainly. But ah, what books we found there!

Those were the days of "real life education" and the dreary Dick and Jane readers that killed the joy of reading for an entire generation. As deprived as we were, we still had these up-to-date textbooks in our classes. But the storage closet was full of old Laidlaw Readers, rich in elves and fairies and wonder. After devouring these, I moved on to the Merrill Graded Literature series and one lucky day discovered a thick volume entitled *Flying Sails*, which I valued so much that I never returned it. The books were falling apart at the seams, but through them I discovered, at age nine or ten, such authors as DeFoe, Blake, Dickens, Shakespeare, Emerson. To be sure, the excerpts were sometimes simplified, but they still contained complex sentences and such delicious words as "dissemble," "impenitent," "sagacious," and "irrepressible," words that were never used on the street where Dick and Jane lived.

Our teachers, too, might have seemed under-qualified by the standards of the colleges of education, since several of them were not college graduates, but they remain fixed in my memory as figures of great knowledge and authority. In retrospect, I wonder how they managed so well. Miss McNeil, my fourth grade teacher, for example, couldn't have been more than twenty when she stepped out of a two-year Normal program and into a classroom that contained (as she put it) "forty-eight pupils and forty-eight squeaky desks." Mrs. Moffitt preserved the gentle competence that made her my favorite teacher through two full sessions of second graders every day. And Mrs. Arnold, who had been teaching forever, had acquired a truly awesome reputation. "You don't know what hard is," the older kids smugly informed the first and second graders, "until you get in the third grade and have Mrs. Arnold. Boy, is she *mean*." And we learned in our turn the full significance of that assessment. You couldn't put anything over on Mrs. Arnold. Just by looking at you, she could tell whether you really had your lessons finished or whether you were just fibbing about it. Throughout the war years, when there were no male teachers in the grade school, she was the school disciplinarian, and would pursue an offender even into the boys' restroom, a fact that led us to post sentries at the door to warn us if she was coming down the hall.

Deprived? Perhaps, but I wouldn't trade my years in a small-town school for the supposedly superior education that my suburban children receive. The value of the experience, however, goes beyond teachers and curriculum. Like the other institutions of the community, our school was a link between the generations. It meant something to me to know that my father had passed through the same halls, sat in the same classrooms, perhaps even the same desk, and had some of the same teachers. Our grade school was originally built as a high school. The building where Dad went to grade school burned down when he was in the fifth grade, and the new building erected to replace it was later converted to a high school. But the high school gymnasium remained in our building, and the high school track meets and baseball games were held on the town square out back. This close proximity of elementary and secondary school is, I understand, also contrary to the recommended practice, but we viewed the closeness of the high school kids as an advantage, as showing us what lay ahead.

These conditions make for continuity, for the repetition of growing-up patterns from generation to generation—for better or worse. Indeed, it is only recently that I have come to realize how exactly the patterns may be repeated. A few years ago, my mother brought me a handful of old UISSCO notebooks—just like the ones I used as a child—in which my father kept a diary during the year 1927, when he was in the eighth and ninth grades. In the diary I found, to my delight, the same adolescent longings and frustrations that I can remember feeling myself, the same hopeless struggles to become an athlete, the same seizures of puppy love. Dad marked off a running track in the cow pasture and trained hard every night, but when he ran against the other boys at school he always lost. He had a crush on a girl named Mildred Miller and saved up his money to buy her a Christmas present, but at a dance just before Christmas she snubbed him in favor of his cousin Bruce Wakefield, so he gave the present to somebody else.

All of this seems very familiar to me, but one incident recorded in the diary, more than any other, gave me a shock of recognition. One day in October, Mr. Bunnell, the shop teacher, sent Dad and Bruce to get some lumber from the storage area under the gymnasium, actually a low, partially excavated crawl space in between the boys' and girls' dressing rooms. Here is the account:

> All went well and the same until we went to Manual Training. We had to go back in the bottom of the building after some boards. I & Bruce went back and old temptation led us to look back thru at the girls undressing. We did and Squeezie *saw* me. I thought *they* would at least keep it a secret, but no!
>
> We got back into shop and began working on our boards when here came Bennett [the principal] and Bunnell. They got us before the whole class. We tried to lie out of it but couldn't. It was awful! Bennett was about to let us out of it tho, but Bunnell said he didn't want us in his class. So Bennett *expelled* us from school.
>
> I had to come clear home to tell Mama. I went and told her a lie too. That'll make it *worse* now.
>
> I left and wandered (and prayed) clear to the foot of the mountain & back. I feel *terrible*! The whole town will know.

The next day, 13 October:

> I dreamed all night about my mishap. Mama almost had to force me to go down town.
>
> Bruce had been allowed back in school by blaming me and when I got there (I and Mama) I got all of the blame and had to confess before Mama. I felt like killing myself!

And for several days afterwards the diary continues to reflect his feeling of scandalous notoriety, as though he were the first and last of sinners. That sense of being uniquely wicked, and uniquely betrayed, is of course common in early adolescence, and that is partly what I recognized in Dad's diary. But there was more. The crawl space under the gym was no longer used for storage when I was in school, and the access door from the boys' dressing room was kept locked. The door was fastened by a simple hasp, however, and the screws could be loosened with the edge of a dime, and "old temptation" was no less active in Poplarhaven in my youth than he had been a generation earlier. Nor had boys become more adept at peeping. As we jostled each other for the best view point, one of the girls heard the sound and looked up.

"You kids!" she squealed, and we felt the weight of doom descending. "There's *boys* in there!"

FOURTEEN

The Girls Across the Valley

It started at dusk on Friday and Saturday nights, the stream of leaded and underslung Fords and Mercuries coming into town from the north, trumpeting their arrival through their muffler cutouts. The boys from Price were coming for our girls.

We resented and envied the boys from Price, resented their intrusion into our territory, envied their assurance, their cars, their clothes, and their success with the girls. But though our resentment produced its share of fistfights in front of the schoolhouse after a basketball game or a dance, it was tempered by the fact that we ourselves were not much interested in the local girls. Like the Price boys, we too preferred to go farther afield for our social life. We didn't very often go to Price, though to do so might have secured a social balance. The Price girls, like the Price boys, seemed too worldly for us, intimidated us by their sophistication, and probably would have scorned the attentions of Poplarhaven hayseeds had we dared to offer them. When we sought girls, we looked on across the valley to the south, to the other Mormon villages of Castle Dale, Orangeville, Ferron, Emery, where there were fresh fields to explore but a lifestyle comfortably similar to our own.

It is difficult to explain why we should have found the girls across the valley so much more interesting than the Poplarhaven girls. Perhaps it was nothing more than excessive familiarity. After sitting together in the same classrooms for ten years, after a hundred birthday parties, playing Red Rover and Jolly Butcher Boy with the same kids, we could only think of the local girls as they were in the skinned-knee and pigtails stage. So we were oblivious to their flowering into adolescence. Only the boys from Price could see it, somewhat to our surprise, while we were fascinated by the girls from other towns, to the amazement of the boys who had grown up with them.

My own interest in girls who were remote from my everyday life goes back as far as I can recall. I regularly fell in love with the leading ladies in the plays my father staged when he taught drama at the high school (for distance in time can be as much an aid to enchantment as distance in space), and I retain an early memory of standing at Grandma Ungerman's gate in Castle Dale and admiring the Johansen girls as they walked by. As a seventh grader, I hiked the six miles to Cleveland one Saturday in hopes of catching a glimpse of Rosalie Carlson, a girl of my own age whose glance could melt a stone. I didn't get to see her, but I gained some solace from gazing at her house for fifteen or twenty minutes. In the ninth grade, the Cleveland girls came to the high school in Poplarhaven and soon lost much of their mystery. From that time on, our romantic dreams attached themselves to the girls who went to South Emery High. We took advantage of every occasion that might lead to new acquaintances, the basketball and baseball games, the track meets and speech meets and music festivals that took us to Ferron or brought the South Emery kids to Poplarhaven. The quarterly LDS stake conferences, which were rotated among the towns in the valley, provided additional opportunities. We used to spend the morning session surveying the congregation to locate the most interesting possibilities. Then during the two-hour lunch break we would try to work our way into the pastel clusters of girls in their Sunday dresses. If we were lucky, we would find somebody to sit beside in the afternoon session.

At sixteen, when we got our driver's licenses, our social life took a great leap forward. We were not as fortunate as the Price boys, who all seemed to have their own cars, low, loud, wearing the perpetual prime coat which proclaimed that the process of customization was still going forward. For the most part, we had to make do with the family car, a dull Dodge or Hudson or Chevy that was all too obviously *not* our own. And even these stodgy sedans were by no means easy to get the use of for an evening. If we had dates, our parents were usually accommodating. But often we did not have dates; we simply wanted to go looking for girls across the valley, and our parents had some difficulty in appreciating the necessity of that, especially since, in their view, there were plenty of nice girls right at home in Poplarhaven.

One of our favorite ploys was to claim that we needed to get our hair cut. We had a barber in Poplarhaven who had seemed perfectly competent in our younger days. But at sixteen we suddenly realized that the only haircuts worthy of the name were to be had from Lee

Peterson over in Castle Dale. And so, when one of us could persuade his parents that his hair had grown too shaggy to endure for another day, we would pile, five or six of us, into the car thus obtained and set out on the ten-mile trip. When we hit Castle Dale we made a quick circuit of the town, honking as we passed the houses of girls we knew. By the time we had finished getting our hair cut, the girls would usually have gathered somewhere to meet us.

They had plenty of time because getting a haircut from Lee Peterson was no short-term project. There were usually several customers already waiting when we arrived, and Lee, though a fine barber and very patient with the finicky demands of teenaged boys, always worked at his own speed. He loved to talk, and indeed the quality of manly conversation was one of the chief attractions of his shop. But the more he talked, the slower he worked, and when he got excited about a point he sometimes stopped altogether and stood scratching his leg with one hand and gesturing with the clippers in the other for emphasis. It might be two hours or more before we got out of the barber shop, but that didn't matter too much; the evening still lay before us, full of promise and discovery.

They were memorable evenings, whether we packed two deep in the car to go park at the Mill Dam, or gathered spontaneously at the home of one of the girls to make popcorn and fudge or honey candy, or, on more formal occasions, drifted cheek-to-cheek around the crowded darkened dance floor with crepe paper streamers overhead while Cal Jewkes intoned the mellow phrases of "That's My Desire":

> To spend a night with you
> In our old rendezvous,
> And reminisce with you. . . .

We wished we could make those evenings last forever, and we made a pretty good stab at it since it was sometimes two or three in the morning before the last girl was kissed on the last doorstep and we began the drive back across the valley toward home, knowing that we would have to face anxious mothers at the end of it, who would scold us for being so late and smell our breath to make sure we hadn't been drinking.

I say we, but in reality I was the most inept of girl-chasers, doomed to be tongue-tied and paralyzed in the presence of a girl I had a crush on. And indeed I could only have a crush on a girl who seemed completely beyond my reach, since romance for me demanded distance and inaccessibility, "the desire of the moth for the star." This attitude led me to actions that are embarrassing to recall. I once sent blank postcards to a certain girl for several months, since what I really wanted to say to her was inexpressible. The anonymous missives made her think someone was threatening her until one of her friends found out the secret. Then she came and sat next to me one night at a dance, a clear indication that she wanted to get acquainted. But instead of asking her to dance I studiously ignored her and carried on an intense discussion with the boy on my other side until somebody else invited her out onto the floor. She ruled my daydreams for more than a year, but in all that time I never once spoke to her.

Strangely enough, though, the girls who were my grand passions are not the ones to whom my thoughts revert most fondly now. Their forms and faces, which I only saw through the filter of romantic fantasy, now seem vague and unreal, while those of some other girls, whom I regarded merely as casual friends, remain vividly present to my imagination. I remember the airiness of summer dresses as a crowd of girls walked arm in arm up the Bench Road on a Sunday afternoon, girls with skinny, coltish limbs, and features still forming, beauty in the bone in process of becoming beauty in the flesh. I remember smiles across cherry Cokes or lemon ironports in Hunter's or Ferron Drug, and deep conversations confiding the heartaches of adolescent love or unraveling the mysteries of the eternal feminine. Their very names retain the resonance of a time when fulfillment seemed to lie in wait somewhere across the valley: Andrea, Ruth, Kaye, Sunny, Barbara, Carol, Doris. I haven't seen any of them in twenty years or more, and I have entirely lost track of most of them, gone from the valley and scattered now. If I could see them once more, I would like to tell them that they were the nicest girls I have ever met, and that, without knowing it at the time, I was a little bit in love with all of them. I still am.

FIFTEEN

The Mill

The mill, which was just up the road from our place, was an irresistible magnet for me as a child, a tall, gray building full of flying belts and spinning wheels and noise. I wasn't allowed to go past the door unless I had come with Dad or Grandpa, or unless old Mr. Sandberg took pity on me and led me up the narrow stairway to explore the wonders of the upper levels. But I could sit on the porch and watch the farmers unload their grain, dumping the gunnysackfuls down a chute where it disappeared behind a heavy grill to be drawn into the mysterious workings. And I could poke around among the weeds out back, where there were rusty cog wheels, broken shafts, and worn-out rollers, or in the gully where the screenings were dumped and where I sometimes found among the chaff and weed seeds great big golden kernels of corn which I carefully picked out and stored in the empty Bull Durham tobacco sacks that I collected from old Bert Westover.

When I was about fifteen years old, I began working at the mill on Saturdays and got to know something of its operations. I discovered that the incoming grain was lifted from the entry chute by elevators—small metal cups attached to a continuous belt—to the top of the mill where it could be channeled through any one of several wooden chutes, some of which led to storage bins, some to the cleaner, with its vibrating screens, and some to the milling machines.

The milling machines stood in rows on all three levels of the building, heavy contraptions made of wood and cast iron with rollers inside that crushed the grain. The wheat passed from one mill to another: the rough mills first, where the kernels were cracked, then to progressively finer mills, which separated out the bran and germ and shorts, leaving fine white flour at the end. Through diverse routes—down chutes and up elevators and down chutes again—different products emerged: whole wheat flour, cracked wheat cereal, germade, and pancake flour mixed to a secret recipe in a rotating drum made from a fifty-gallon barrel.

Except for the chopping mills and feed mixers, which stood in a shed attached to the main building and had their own motors, everything in the mill was run by a large electric motor in the cellar. A heavy belt connected the motor to shafts that ran the length of the mill on each level. From these shafts, other belts on pulleys of various sizes ran the different machines.

In the years I worked there, I got acquainted with every part of the mill: the storeroom with its rich, floury aroma, the cellar with thick rock walls and piers, the place where the steam engine had once been housed, and which was now used to store empty gunnysacks. (The mill was originally run by waterpower and then steam before the electric motor was installed, and it still bore traces of each successive era.) I clung perilously to catwalks above storage bins that looked bottomless in the dim light and descended ladders into them to shovel out the last grain that would not feed itself into the augers under the floor. When the bin was empty and swept clean, I spread lime in the corners, to keep the vermin out, before it was refilled. The air in the deep bins was hot and motionless and full of dust and lime that seared the membranes of my nose and throat. I sometimes lifted heavy feed sacks until my shoulders felt numb. Most of the time, though, I spent packaging cereals and pancake flour in a routine that became automatic: fill, tamp, fold, paste, stack.

The one thing I never did, and always wanted to do, was bag flour. The bagging apparatus was a wonderful assemblage of gears, platforms, counter-weights, pedals, and levers that stood near the counter where the mill's business was transacted, and near the stove that glowed red in the wintertime, the sole island of warmth in the entire building. While I shivered in my coat back at the cereal hopper with flour-and-water paste congealing on my stiff fingers, the miller worked in comfort by the stove, filling the flour sacks that bore the proud legend, "Castle Valley's Best," sewing them closed, and stacking them as high as they could go on the hand truck, then wheeling them into the storeroom to await the Thursday delivery to stores throughout the valley.

The mill was—and is—a relic of the early days in Poplarhaven, the oldest commercial or public building still in use. It was built in the early 1890s as a cooperative venture, set on a sturdy rock foundation and framed with timbers hewn from the ponderosa pines in the lower canyons. It was operated by a succession of millers, with uneven success, until about 1919, when Olaf Sandberg, who had learned the miller's trade in his native Sweden, purchased the mill and moved to Poplarhaven with a family of big, strong sons. When I knew him, old Mr. Sandberg had turned the management of the mill over to his eldest son, Willard, but he still spent much of his time at the mill, talking with the customers in a high-pitched voice and teasing young boys by poking at them with his cane, one of a large collection that he had cut over the years from the thicket along the canal. He still had his Swedish accent and his high spirits, though he was deaf from a lifetime of mill noise and bent from lifting innumerable sacks.

Olaf Sandberg lived across the road from the mill in a house whose pitched roof and pleasant situation reminded me of a storybook cottage. Mrs. Sandberg, who was of German ancestry, was as serious in manner as her husband was jovial. Her response to any piece of news was to get a concerned wrinkle in her forehead and say, "Oh my!" in deep solemn tones that suggested she was aware of all the misfortune in the world. It was not until many years later that I realized there had been a strain of wry humor beneath her solemnity. She kept an immaculate house and yard, sent in delicious meals to her neighbors when they were sick, and served as a one-woman test kitchen for the mill's products. No batch of flour was sent out to the stores unless she was satisfied with the bread it made. I wonder, though, whether any flour could have failed in her hands, for although I grew up on good homemade bread I have never eaten any that could compare with hers, warm from the oven, sliced thick, heavy with butter.

Willard Sandberg was my boss, and I was always afraid of him. He had piercing eyes and a businesslike moustache, and a brusque manner. As a young man, he had worked for a time in a New York bank, returning home to the family business at the onset of the Great Depression. He would really have preferred the life of an urban executive. After work and on Sundays, he used to dress up in a suit and tie, and then, since there was no place to go, walked restlessly up and down in front of his house on Main Street until it was time to go over to the movie theater that he operated in partnership with Ted Nielson. But while the miller's trade might not have been the life he would have chosen, he was good at it. He could handle any task, from hefting the heaviest sacks, to repairing the machinery (though not without some cussing), to managing the finances. He could bite a single kernel of wheat and tell you how much protein it contained, and he was, in addition to everything else, the most fastidious man I have ever known. He always kept a push broom close at hand, and you could have eaten off the floor of the mill at any time. Nothing irritated him more—not even a broken belt at a busy time—than a customer who failed to wipe his feet at the door.

Virtually every community used to have a flour mill which provided food for man and beast and materials for flour-sack dishtowels —and even homemade underwear. Very few remain in operation today, probably not more than four or five in the state of Utah. Some survive as feed mills only. Some have been adapted to other uses, such as restaurants. Others remain as picturesque ruins. The town mill belongs to a vanishing landscape, along with the old barns, the pioneer meetinghouses, and the tall, straight rows of Lombardy poplars. It pleases me that, with so many things gone from the town of my childhood, the old mill remains, and remains operational, still whirring and clanking, still transforming the wheat grown on the little patchwork fields into products for the morning "mush," the daily bread, the miracle of sustenance which I can never take for granted because I grew up neighbor to a mill.

SIXTEEN

Harvest Home

Harvest season, in our valley, was not only the culmination but also the accompaniment of the growing season. The first radishes from the garden were a sign that spring had really, finally arrived, and many a meal that I can remember was made up of bread and butter and radishes, or, a little later, bread and butter and green onions. When the peas came on, we could have lived in the garden, and after the peas there were immature carrots and potatos to dig and prepare in a rich cream sauce. In August the sweet corn and tomatoes came on, to continue the feast clear until first frost.

You could more or less count on a garden. Orchards were more chancy, and by the time I came along people had pretty much abandoned serious fruit-growing in our valley, except for a few places in the canyon mouths where the air movement helped avert the late frosts. Many town lots still had a little orchard patch, but there were spaces in the rows where trees had died and not been replaced. The remaining trees were thick and gnarled below, dense above with unpruned growth. In my view, an orchard was well worth having even if it never bore fruit, simply as a sort of private forest to play in. And there were good years when the old trees brought forth an Edenic abundance. Then we ate green apples with puckery relish, carrying a fragment of rock salt in our pockets throughout the early weeks of summer so that we could alternate licks of salt with bites of apple. At least once a year we were sure to overdo it and suffer the agonies of green apple bellyache. In midsummer, the apricots came on, followed by the Yellow Transparent apples, and daily dessert was apple crunch swimming in fresh cream. A few weeks later, another apple ripened in Grandpa's orchard whose identity I have never been able to discover, a small apple with orange and yellow stripes and flesh like ambrosia. Fall brought crisp Jonathans to be stored in a bin in the cellar, and pears to be bottled. Mother and Grandma preferred Bartlett pears for canning, but I favored the grainy sweetness of the big

Flemish Beauties, and so did the wasps that congregated under the tree to gorge themselves on the windfalls. Peaches rarely survived the spring frosts, but when they bore there was one small, white-fleshed peach whose skin could be stripped off in one piece and whose flesh literally melted in your mouth.

So great was the abundance of fruit in some seasons that it overflowed the orchard boundaries and spread out around the town: mulberries overhanging the sidewalks, white, purple, and black; thickets of plums growing untended around abandoned cabins, too tart, almost, to eat but wonderful for jelly; gooseberry bushes in the dooryard, black and golden currants along the fencelines, and red, alumy bullberries out by the creek. Up the canyon there were chokecherries, and, farther up, elderberries, and on the foothills pine nuts, a gathering of which would stain your hands with sticky gum that took days to wear off—but not as long as the stain from the black walnuts that were gathered by the gunnysackful from the lawn. Scarcely any of this produce had commercial value. Everything was too small or too wormy, too uneven in color or too lively in flavor for the bland preferences of the supermarket, but what a variety of sensations for the palate! What lessons, too, in the general conditions of existence, where no satisfaction comes unalloyed. We learned early that there are plenty of good bites left in an apple after the worm is finished with it. You just have to take them a bit carefully, that's all.

While the fruit matured in its rich succession, the patches of grain interspersed among the hayfields gradually took on their ripening colors, a silver acre of oats here, three golden acres of wheat there, and a patch of bearded barley over by the Cox place. After the second crop of hay was harvested, the binder would be brought out of its resting place, greased up, and fitted with its canvas conveyor belt to begin reaping the grain.

A binder is a wonderfully gangly machine, a Rube Goldberg assemblage of arms and pulleys and gears and levers improbably flailing its way across the field and, surprisingly, actually doing its job, leaving a trail of neatly bound bundles as it goes. Then the bundles are gathered in shocks (called "stooks" in some regions) to dry. Shocking is a skill that I could never master. It looked easy enough when Grandpa gathered a bundle under each arm and plumped them down so that the stem end lodged firmly against the ground and kept the bundles upright, their tops leaning together. But my first pair invariably toppled over before I could add other bundles to the shock, so I had to content myself with adding bundles to Grandpa's shocks.

Grandpa liked to shock grain at night when it was cool and the harvest moon cast a shimmery blue light. It always seemed strange to me to work in the field after dark, and I preferred the autumn afternoons when the land lay under a golden haze. I liked to crawl into the long, narrow tunnel that ran down the middle of a shock and lie there against the ground, leisurely breaking apart a head of wheat, blowing off the hulls, and munching the kernels while I breathed in the rich, ripe smell of earth and harvest.

When the shocks had stood in the field long enough to grow thoroughly dry, it was time for hauling. Hauling grain was very different from hauling hay. The pitchforks were narrower and the loading and stacking operations more intricate. A load of grain could only be so high, and so could a stack. The stacks were formed of concentric circles of bundles, all with heads toward the center of the stack and stems pointed outward. The pitchers tossed the bundles one by one to the stackers, who caught them on their pitchforks and turned them deftly to place them just right, building the stack layer by layer until the self-thatched cone was complete. There was never any question, as there was with hay, whether you could raise the stack higher or put on one more load. When a grain stack was finished it was finished, and a single additional bundle would merely slide off. There was nothing to do but begin another stack next to the first one. By the end of hauling, there would be several stacks clustered together west of the barn, looking like giant beehives.

They might stand there for several weeks, for threshing did not normally begin until all other harvesting was complete. Then each farm must wait its turn as the threshers made their rounds. Threshing day was the climax of the harvest season, and when the threshers reached our neighborhood we used to count farms and grain stacks anxiously, hoping that they would reach our place on a Saturday so that we would have the entire day free to enjoy the operation.

Our threshing was done by Neil Howard and his crew. Neil Howard had lost both legs in an accident when he was five years old, and he got around on a single short, thick artificial leg and a pair of crutches. I never thought of him as handicapped, however, for he could do almost anything. He ran a sawmill and a farm, in addition to his threshing machine. He was remarkably agile on his crutches, which served as handy extensions of his arms to knock loose a clogged chute or shove a misaligned belt back onto its proper track. What he could not do himself, he directed his helpers to do, with sharp, no-nonsense commands that were instantly obeyed. To my young perceptions, Neil Howard's loss had its positive side, for though he was massively built he stood at a child's height, bringing a man's work down to our level, as it were. Occasionally, when everything was running properly, he would pause for a little while, drape his arms easily over his crutches, tuck a pinch of snuff inside his lip, and chat with us kids in his gruff, friendly way. I have never in my life felt more important than when Neil Howard stopped to talk with me.

No other machine is quite as mechanical as a thresher. It has every kind of motion there is. The long leather drive belt goes smack-smack, and its polished surface glints in the sunlight as it moves. The feed conveyor creaks as it carries the bundles of grain into the ferocious jaws, which chomp and grind. The straw chute howls like a tornado and can be raised and lowered and cranked in and out and turned this way and that by means of a clever set of wheels and racks and pinions. Everywhere pulleys spin, separators oscillate, and the whole monstrous mechanism teeters and vibrates in a most satisfactory way, all to produce the precious trickle of grain to be caught in gunnysacks and stacked on the wagon.

The noise and motion go on at a constant tempo, while the crew must work at the machine's pace, forking in the bundles, adjusting the straw chute to build the stack, changing sacks on the grain spout. It is a harder and more unremitting labor than haying, and so there is a greater sense of relief when dinnertime comes and the thresher is shut down, leaving a loud silence ringing in your ears. The crew troops toward the hydrant to sluice off as much chaff as possible, then files into the house, where the dining room table has been extended to its utmost. "Feeding the threshers" was a proverbial expression for woman's work at its heaviest, and I suspect that Grandma did not look forward to threshing day quite as eagerly as I did.

When the threshing was over, the straw stack made a fine slippery slide for a while. When Grandpa wasn't around, we would climb onto the roof of the sheep shed and throw ourselves onto the stack, scooting down its side to the ground. After one or two autumn storms, the straw lost its slickness and the stack grew stable. The cows and sheep would nibble at it throughout the winter, creating caves that we could play in. The bins in the inside-out granary were full to the rafters, and a load or two of wheat had been hauled to the mill for the winter's flour. With the harvest completed, Grandpa could turn his attention to the forty-days' rain of leaves that had accumulated on the lawn and that the grandchildren had piled into great mounds to jump on or run through or bury ourselves in. We hauled the leaves in bushel baskets to a place by the ditchbank, where Grandpa burned them. They produced little flame but yielded a thin blue smoke that smelled wonderful and spread in horizontal bands across the valley, blending with the haze that hung over the tawny fields. That was the season for "playing out" in the lengthening evenings, for bonfires on the ridge by the graveyard, with potatoes roasting in the embers while we played hide-and-seek in the hollows.

"Nothing is nicer," Grandpa used to say, "than a full barn and a full granary." He might have said a full cellar too, for the rows of bottled fruit loomed on the shelves in the dim light, and the aroma of apples filled the nostrils. We could sit down at the dinner table knowing where everything on it had come from, and the process by which it had been prepared. We had before us and around us tangible evidence of the interconnection of things, of tilling, and seedtime, and harvest, of process and product, work and reward. Abundance is what remained when the threshing was done and the mellow Utah autumn slid gradually into winter, abundance in the storehouse for man and beast, evidence that we reap as we have sown. And abundance in the memory which lasts long after the barn and granary are empty hulks, for sometimes we also reap where others have sown.

SEVENTEEN

Roundup

Bib overalls were among the great trials of my early life. My father held the firm conviction that it was unhealthy to suspend one's trousers from the waist. The shoulders were meant to carry weight, he said, and anyone who tried to do the job by cinching a belt around his middle ran the risk of damaging his innards. Dad wore suspenders with his dress trousers and bib overalls when he worked outside, as did Grandpa. But Grandpa's overalls, at least, were blue while Dad purchased for himself and for me striped overalls toward which I developed such an aversion that it still amazes me to see anybody wearing them by choice. All of my friends and all of the older boys that I admired wore Levis, either with wide leather belts and decorative buckles or else beltless and hanging low on their hips. The only other boy in my class who wore bib overalls was one who had been held back in school. He was twice as big as anyone else, spent recesses strolling alone around the school grounds with his hands tucked inside his bib, and was liable at unexpected moments to begin barking like a dog or wailing like a siren.

I hated bib overalls not merely because they marked me as different from the other kids but because they were so totally out of keeping with the image of myself I liked to cultivate. My goal in life was to be a rancher. I dreamed of discovering, somewhere out in the desert, a valley green with spring-fed meadows and surrounded by red rock walls with one secret entrance that only I would know. There I would develop my herd of prize Hereford cattle, and build barns and corrals and a big ranch house with a wide veranda, and ride around all day on the horse that I would capture from the wild desert bands. I would always wear cowboy boots and Levis and a plaid Pendleton shirt with pearl buttons.

The Levis and boots and shirts were seen regularly enough around Poplarhaven, but none of the men there quite fit my image of the rancher. Instead, they were farmers who also ran cattle on the range. A few families, McElprangs, Guymons, Brashers, had fairly large holdings and trailed their cattle from the desert to the foothills to the high plateaus and back again each year, but even they spent most of the time tilling their fields. Many families had only twenty or thirty head of stock on the range, hardly enough to qualify them as cattle barons.

There was one time of the year, however, when the farmers were transformed into genuine cowmen and Poplarhaven took on the look of a real Western town. That was the annual roundup each October, when the cattle were brought down from the mountain. Each farmer with stock on the range was obligated to provide some horse- and manpower for the series of organized drives that covered all parts of the range. Over a period of several days, riders would comb the meadows and hillsides of Gentry Hollow, McHaddon Flat, Crandall Canyon, Tie Fork, gathering the scattered animals into larger groups and working them down toward the bottom of the canyon where they formed large herds for the drive to the valley. The herds were brought to the public corral, where each farmer could come to pick out his own animals and take them home.

The public corral was just down the road from our place. It was built of thick aspen logs and consisted of two large enclosures and numerous smaller pens with connecting chutes. In the large enclosures were water troughs made from hollowed-out pine trunks into which a constant trickle of water flowed, producing bright green moss and overflowing to form puddles where we could catch pollywogs in the spring. The public corral was an interesting place in any season, but at roundup time it was irresistible. A cloud of dust hung over it, and there were continual comings and goings. Even in the night I could hear from my bedroom the chorus of lowing cattle. The corral lay there in my way as I walked home from school, a lure from which neither parental threats nor a boy's after-school hunger could divert me.

It was an unspoken rule that nobody simply came and got his cows and went home again. Instead, you had to sit awhile on the top pole of the fence with your hat brim pulled down low over your eyes, spitting occasionally into the dust, and discussing with your neighbors such issues as whether the cattle had come off the range looking good or poor, whether you could break even on the price of weaner calves, and whether Franklin D. Roosevelt was the farmer's salvation or his destruction. I was sure that if I weren't wearing bib overalls I could have sat a fence as well as any of them, squinting at the sun to tell the time of day and spitting between my teeth as they did. As it was, I crept as close to them as I dared and listened to their conversations. The real show, however, went on in the corral itself, where Frank Robbins directed the working of the cattle, standing a little in his stirrups, holding the reins easily in one hand while he cut in and out of the herd, spotting which calf belonged to which cow, shouting orders to the men who ran the gates. Once I got the chance to run the gate as some animals were being transferred from one pen to another, but I botched the job, letting the wrong cow push through before I could shut the gate and drawing a sharp rebuke. Even then I didn't leave the corral but tried to make myself as inconspicuous as possible while I continued to watch the goings on.

The only thing that could draw me away while daylight remained was the news that a new herd was coming down the canyon. Then I would climb to the top of Sandberg's Hill to watch for the arrival. It was a great sight when they crested the ridge above Reed Brasher's, maybe two hundred head, a shifting, flowing mass of reddish-brown with riders spaced around the perimeter of the herd and dogs running low to the ground to nip at the heels of the stragglers. The concerted lowing of the cows and bawling of the calves was punctuated by the strident bellowing of the bulls. I would run along in advance of the herd to be on hand when it was turned in to the corral to mingle with the remnant of earlier drives. The bulls would paw up the dust and rush at the fences to shake their horns at the men or snort challenges at other bulls in neighboring pens. It was a scene I never tired of.

Grandpa used to make a daily trip to the public corral to bring home the six or eight or ten head of his stock that had arrived since the day before. Cows just down from the mountain were wily and independent, much harder to drive than the placid animals that were kept in the pastures at home. I remember one big brockle-face cow, half Durham, that sometimes evaded the roundup altogether and wintered on the range, coming home perhaps the following year, wilder than ever. The continual movement of such animals through the streets of town generated a fair amount of excitement, requiring numerous mad dashes to head them off at cross streets and considerable swearing sometimes to make them see an open gate.

The cattle were customarily kept in the barnyards for a week or two, so the entire town was filled with their sounds and smells. When the roundup was substantially complete, families would gather for branding day, an occasion that remains in the memory as a vivid melange of acrid smoke, bawling calves, rope burns, and jokes about Rocky Mountain oysters. Families with winter range on the desert would then wean the calves and take the cows out to forage on shadscale around Cedar Mountain or along the San Rafael River, while those, like us, who wintered at home turned their animals onto the harvested fields to graze off the residue of the crops before beginning to feed them hay.

At about age ten, I refused to wear bib overalls any longer and succeeded in getting my parents to buy me Levis. But my life as a cowboy remained mostly imaginary. I never learned to handle a horse very well and never rode on the roundup. Dad rode occasionally, and once when I was perhaps five or six years old Mother and I accompanied him to the base camp in the canyon. Pete McElprang and Ira Marshall, experienced cowmen, camped with us, and I was tremendously impressed at the professionalism of their outfits. They had chaps and spurs and thick bedrolls of homemade quilts and packed their grub in wooden powder boxes. I will never forget the morning glow on Pete McElprang's face when he came back from washing in the icy water of the creek, or the smell of bacon and eggs frying in the big black skillet over the open fire, or the natural way the men swung into their saddles and rode away up Tie Fork after breakfast. Indeed, when I think of real men I still think of the old cowmen of Poplarhaven, of Pete McElprang, Frank Robbins, Iver Truman, Reub Brasher, Miller Black. There were giants in the earth in those days.

EIGHTEEN

Politics

Adriaan Nagelvoort, as I have since learned by looking him up in *American Men of Science*, was a consulting chemist and chemical engineer of considerable reputation. But I remember him best as the man who could pull his thumb off. Whenever he came to our house, he would obligingly repeat the trick for me, slowly drawing the last joint of his thumb away from the base, then, as though to replace it before the bleeding started, shoving it quickly back into place and peering blandly through his glasses while I examined the joint for any sign of injury. It was quite an amazing trick.

Mr. Nagelvoort had come to Poplarhaven to develop a process for extracting fossil resin from the local coal. He built a lab and settling tanks at the mouth of Deer Creek and pursued the project intermittently for several years, periodically interrupting his work to replenish his funds by working for a mining firm in South America. Any stranger coming into our close-knit Mormon community at that period would have been a novelty, but the Nagelvoorts were especially interesting. They built a New England-style saltbox and painted it bright yellow, which contrasted strikingly with the earthen tones of our brick and adobe houses. Mr. Nagelvoort sported tweeds and flannels and sometimes a pair of knickers, and he carried a walking stick when he strolled uptown to get his mail. Mrs. Nagelvoort wore high-styled dresses that she purchased on her visits to New York, and her pepper-and-salt hair and swarthy complexion led some people to suspect that she might be Jewish, like Dr. Turman in Castle Dale. Their speech was quite unlike our southern Utah twang, but they were also different from each other. Mr. Nagelvoort, who was originally from Nebraska and had graduated from the University of Michigan, had an easy, melodious voice while his wife spoke rapidly in a clipped, eastern accent, punctuated by quick hand gestures. She was a competent, if rather dramatic, pianist who was often called upon to perform at community events, and many of us kids took piano lessons from her.

The Nagelvoorts claimed to have no religious affiliation, but that seemed hardly credible to us, and there was perennial speculation about what they *really* were. Were they Jewish? Were they Catholic? Some of my classmates referred to Mr. Nagelvoort as "the mad scientist," though nothing could less resemble madness than his mild, confident manner. He did display a few oddities, though, in addition to his dress. For example, he had a habit of replying to casual observations about the weather by saying, "It's a fine day for Republicans!" Some people in our strongly Democratic town took this as an insult, though he always smiled pleasantly as he said it.

I didn't mind Mr. Nagelvoort's political remark. Our family was among the small group of Republicans who were striving to sustain the cause during the difficult period of the Roosevelt years. That is one reason why we were friends with the Nagelvoorts. It was a lonely time for Republicans, and we were glad for whatever political companionship we could find.

I first became aware of the political climate of our town on election day in 1944. I remember looking up from play on the schoolhouse lawn during recess and seeing the flag in front of the meetinghouse across the street, where the polls were.

"Hey," I said to the other first graders playing around me, "it's election day. Let's go vote for Dewey."

There was a painful silence. Then Claude Johnson said, "No, let's vote for Roosevelt. He's The President!"

We wrestled to determine the better candidate, and Dewey lost that contest too. I was convinced, however, that it wasn't a fair fight. Claude got an easy hold on me, and Mother maintained that Roosevelt had been in office for so long that people had forgotten how to vote for anybody else. When he died not long after the election, we felt vindicated. But Roosevelt's demise brought Harry Truman to the White House, and though we found his Missouri accent less offensive than Roosevelt's speech he was obviously a man of no refinement, unworthy of the office. Thomas E. Dewey, on the other hand, was a very dignified man. His campaign biography had a prominent place on our bookshelf, and I often took the volume down to admire the photograph on the dust jacket. Dewey somewhat resembled my father. They were both short, well-groomed men with black hair and neatly trimmed moustaches. I thought Dewey looked just fine and couldn't understand why my classmates made fun of his appearance.

Every week when I went to my piano lesson, Mrs. Nagelvoort spent part of the time talking politics—when she wasn't reminding me to keep my fingers arched as I played so that my hands wouldn't tire too easily when I became a concert pianist. She was always outraged at Truman's latest offenses against good breeding and never failed to point out that Dewey would be conducting things much differently if he were The President. We both knew that it was only a matter of time.

I got deeply involved in the 1948 campaign, listening avidly to the Republican National Convention on the radio, helping Dad tack posters on telephone poles, and going to school with my shirt laden with buttons. The high point of my political career came when I heard Dewey speak in the Salt Lake Tabernacle. Because Dad was the county Republican chairman (a post for which there was little competition), we had seats on the rostrum which gave us a fine view of the candidate's statesmanlike back as he spoke. When the speech was over, Dad hustled me into the aisle where Dewey would pass. Suddenly, out of the crush of bodies, the great man appeared before me, impeccable in a navy blue suit. He stuck out a hand and grasped mine, saying that he was always glad to meet an up-and-coming Republican. Then his entourage swept him up the aisle and out of sight. When we got back to the hotel room, Mother suggested that I shouldn't wash the hand, a course that I seriously considered for a while.

I also saw Truman in person that year. His whistle-stop campaign brought him through our remote valley, and school was dismissed so that we could go to Price and hear him speak. I went despite my dislike for the man because, as Grandma said, he was The President in spite of everything, and also because I liked trains. I remember the sight of the big diesel engines coming in from the east and the excited buzz in the crowd as the train slowed to a halt. We had to wait for several minutes before the energetic man in the rimless glasses emerged onto the rear platform and waved to us.

Truman began by saying that he had been looking out of the train windows as it approached the town and had seen one of the lovely garden spots of America. This brought a ripple of laughter even from the Democrats in the crowd (who were of course the great majority, Price being an even more strongly Democratic town than Poplarhaven). Anyone who has traveled by rail or road from Grand

Junction to Price knows that it is an extremely barren region. Later, Dad suggested charitably that perhaps the train was crossing Kansas the last time Truman looked out the window, but the whole episode merely confirmed my conviction of the man's insincerity and incompetence. I waited eagerly for the election that would sweep him out of office and Dewey in. On election night, I caught the early returns on the radio and went to bed confident that we were winning. My parents, gathered at the Nagelvoorts' house with a few friends for a victory party, heard the turning of the tide after midnight. Mother reported that when the California returns began to come in, Mrs. Nagelvoort anxiously crossed herself. So that question, too, was settled.

American politics have changed greatly since 1948, when a ten-year-old boy living in an obscure southern Utah village could see both major presidential candidates in person and shake hands with one of them. I have changed too, losing my childhood political convictions, perhaps because I now live in a Republican town and cannot bear to vote with the majority. (I can imagine Mr. Nagelvoort shaking his head and clicking his tongue in mild disapproval.) I can understand now what people meant when they said that Dewey looked like the little man on the wedding cake. Some prejudices die hard, and I still cannot see the greatness that many people ascribe to FDR. But my opinion of Harry Truman has risen, even if he couldn't tell the difference between a garden and a desert.

The thing I admire the most about Truman's presidency is the way he left it. When the Eisenhower inauguration was over, Harry and Bess simply got into their car and drove home to Missouri. When you consider how many millions of the taxpayers' dollars it has taken to get ex-presidents out of Washington in recent years, that modest transition is enough to make anybody long for the good old days.

III

NINETEEN

The Girl Who Danced
with Butch Cassidy

My earliest recollection of Retty Mott is of hurrying past her house on my way home from school. I kept to the other side of the road and hurried past because my older cousins had told me that she chased people. One time she had jumped out from behind a tree in her yard and hit Max Peterson with a fire shovel. She chased him clear to the end of the block, hitting him with the fire shovel all the way, or so my cousins said, and it did not occur to me to doubt their stories or to wonder what Max Peterson was doing in her yard.

I could easily believe the stories about Retty Mott because she reminded me of the witches on the Halloween decorations, with her angular frame, her sharp features, and the long, nervous fingers. She was the same age as my grandmother, but not at all grandmotherly. The other old women in Poplarhaven wore muted print dresses and black coats and kept their hair tucked in with tortoise shell combs. Retty Mott, summer or winter, marched downtown in a straw hat with a floppy brim and no crown, so that her wiry gray hair came straggling out through the top, and a flowered wrapper beneath which it was rumored she wore no underclothing. She never came to church, not even on Mother's Day when even the Jack Mormons came out and we had to use the spare sacrament trays. By the time I knew her, she had been married twice, so Mott was probably not her legal name. But the childhood nickname that she hated had become her only identity: Retty Mott, the two names indivisible, a label unalterable by her wishes or by the law, to which no husband's name could be added and no title affixed, not Miss Mott, or Mrs. Mott, and certainly not Sister Mott.

When I became as old as my cousins had been, I learned what they had known before me: the pleasures of teasing Retty Mott. We did it mostly on summer nights, when the drugstore had closed but we weren't ready yet to go home. After we had stood for a while on the corner by Maurice Jensen's store waiting to see if any girls would come by, someone would suggest that we go tease Retty Mott. Then we would drift in a group up the dark street toward the little frame house under the locust trees, our loud talk fading as we drew closer until there was only the occasional scraping of a shoe on the graveled road against the background music of the crickets and toads. Finally, when we were right in front of the house, there came the electric moment when somebody (it was usually Ferd Nichols) suddenly screamed, "Retty Mott!" and the fun began.

That first shout always caught the rest of us unprepared and sent us running, to regroup on the next block. Now came the second assault, with its element of danger. She might be waiting for us now, hiding behind a tree with her fire shovel, or even with her father's old Colt .45, which she was said to keep somewhere in the house. We kept our muscles tensed to break and run as we crept closer. At last, when we could bear the strain no longer, we shouted again, not a single voice this time but a rising chorus. "Retty Mott! Retty Mott!" We yelled the name over and over. Then we proceeded to songs and chants:

> Some like 'em hot,
> Some like 'em cold,
> But who wants Retty Mott
> Seventy years old?

If she still did not respond, we grew bolder. We threw rocks at the roof, flinging them high in the air and waiting for the sound when they struck the weathered shingles and rattled down to the eaves. Or we tossed pebbles at the windows, but very gently so as not to break them. We didn't want to cause any damage. The more daring among us (not I!) might dart up onto the porch and hammer on the door with their fists then sprint back to the safety of the group. We kept it up until Retty Mott came rushing out of the house, screaming obscenities at us, with her wrapper flapping about her skinny legs. Sometimes we were satisfied then and went home, but sometimes we couldn't bear to end the fun and we went back again and again until Hawkshaw Rowley, the town marshall, came and chased us away.

"Somebody ought to horsewhip those little Mormon shits," Retty Mott said to my grandmother one day downtown while I stood a few feet away with a sack of groceries in my arms and my eyes fixed on some object in the indefinite distance. Grandma said, "Now, now, now . . ."

We called it *teasing* Retty Mott, and we saw no harm in it because she was a rawboned old woman with twitching hands and a shrill voice, and because she seemed to have nothing in common with us. And yet she had been born just two miles out of town, in a log house by the creek. Ezra Mott was one of the cattlemen who brought their herds into the valley in the early 1870s, before the town was settled. The country was all open in those days, and soon there were half a dozen ranches strung along the creek, stations on the trail between the summer meadows of the Wasatch Plateau and the winter range in the San Rafael Desert. When the Mormon settlers arrived, they laid out a townsite and dug irrigation canals. The ranchers came mostly from Mormon stock themselves, but had drifted out of the society. Thus there came to be two different ways of life in the valley, the village culture of Poplarhaven, built around the meetinghouse on the town square, and the free and easy life of the ranchers on the creek and of the cowboys who drifted in and out to work the herds, carrying everything they owned in their saddlebags. The cattlemen picked up their mail and bought supplies in town. They patronized Silas Walker's store, which had a lean-to back room for card games, while most of the townspeople traded at the Coop. Men from the ranches and men from the town could often be seen passing the time of day together, squatting on their heels by a sunny wall. And when there were church socials in the Relief Society Hall, the cowboys often came and danced with the town girls while the town boys watched sullenly from the sidelines. But if there were connecting links, there were also dividing lines. When a drunk cowboy drowned while attempting to cross the creek during high water one spring, the townspeople would not allow him to be buried in the graveyard, for it was said that when he was warned against trying to cross the stream he had uttered a curse and defied the Lord.

The cowboy's grave was still visible when I was a boy, just outside the graveyard fence, close to yet separated from the graves inside. It was marked by a wooden plank set upright in the ground, but the carved inscription had long since worn away and the plank itself was so brittle that the slightest push would have broken it off. On Decoration Day, when the graveyard was bright with peonies and bridal wreath, we kids would sometimes pick wildflowers from the hill and put them on the stranger's grave.

From the graveyard you can see the creek—a harmless trickle of tepid water when we used to go out there in the summers to swim in the holes and fish for suckers—and beyond it the old Mott place which was the stranger's destination, as it was the destination of most of the cowboys who drifted through Poplarhaven in the early days. The ranch house still stood on a rise above the creek, an empty shell. Sometimes, when the fish weren't biting, we would walk up and explore the ruins, stepping cautiously on the rotten floorboards and looking out of the gaps where the windows had been, trying to imagine ourselves in the world of the westerns that we saw at the Thursday night picture show. We searched in the brush along the creek for the location of the cabin where the cowboys bunked. Once we found some flat rocks that might have been foundation piers, and another time Ernie Broadbent picked up a pocketknife embedded in rust.

According to local legend, Butch Cassidy and Elza Lay had spent the winter of 1896–97 at the Mott ranch while they were planning the Castle Gate payroll robbery. The robbery was the most exciting episode in Poplarhaven's history, even though the event itself took place in a coal camp some thirty miles away. I heard the story retold so many times during my boyhood that I came to think of it as something I had lived through myself, as though I had witnessed everything, but at a certain distance from the events. From a vantage point on the ledges above Castle Gate, I can still visualize the two men slouched on their horses as the Rio Grande train winds down the narrow canyon and chuffs to a halt. The paymaster and his assistant emerge from the baggage car carrying several heavy sacks and cross the road to the mine office above the company store. As they disappear up the stairs, one of the men on horseback dismounts easily and follows them, his hat pulled low over his eyes.

I see the escape as though from a greater height, a panoramic view taking in the whole sweep of the valley. There is a sudden stir in the street as the outlaws ride out of town, dropping a bag filled with silver coins as they go. They pause momentarily to cut the telegraph line in the canyon narrows, then move away from the railroad track, making a wide arc to the west across the mouth of Spring Canyon and Gordon Creek, then aiming for Pinnacle Butte, and then curving southward across the Washboard Flat, where they stop again to cut the telegraph line to Poplarhaven and to change to the fresh horses they had taken from the Mott ranch and stationed there the previous day. With renewed speed they ride on past Bull Hollow, around Cedar Mountain, and down Buckhorn Draw to the San Rafael River. Once across the river they go at an easier pace toward Robbers' Roost on the wedge of rock between the Green River and the Dirty Devil.

I can see the scene in Poplarhaven that day with equal vividness but at closer range. There is a buckboard tied at the hitching rack in front of Walker's store, where the telegraph was. (I remember the hitching rack; a long pine pole fastened at each end to a cedar post, it remained between two thick-trunked poplar trees into my own life-time, long after the store with its false front and plank porch had been demolished.) On the seat of the buckboard sits a girl of fifteen, a wiry tomboy in a calico dress. Her features are strained, and she is biting her lower lip. Nearby stands a boy with my grandfather's face. Perhaps it is through his ears that I hear the two men jawing in the midst of the crowd on the porch.

Bishop Hardy is saying, "Lordamighty, Ez, didn't you know who they was?" For he has just learned that the two cowboys who wintered at the Mott ranch and who went by the names of Tom Gilbert and Bert Fowler have robbed the Castle Gate payroll.

"How the hell am I supposed to know about every hand that drifts into my place?" says Ezra Mott, his voice, unacquainted with the need to reach into the back corners of the meetinghouse where the boys play mumblety-peg during meeting, lower than the bishop's. "You seen them yourself, here in town. They wasn't any different than anybody else."

I have seen a photograph of Ezra Mott, taken at about that period. It is a profile shot of a man sitting ramrod straight on a big horse, dressed in a black coat with a flat black hat pulled down over his eyes and a thick moustache. I have also seen a photo of Bishop Hardy, taken many years later. He is seated with his surviving wife and a flock of children and grandchildren, the bearded patriarch amid his tribe. The eyes look straight out at you from under the bushy white brows.

"Don't you give me a hard time, Bishop," Ezra Mott is saying in that low voice. "I'm out a damn sight more than any of you. They took my best horses, didn't they?"

"Well, well," Bishop Hardy says in a conciliatory tone, "they're running for the Roost, sure as you're born. You get some of your people, and we'll try to head them off at the Draw."

An hour later a dozen men on horseback are milling about in the street with Bishop Hardy and Ezra Mott jostling for position at the head.

"Tell your ma I won't be home for supper," the bishop shouts to a small boy in patched overalls.

The boy shouts back. "You was eating at Aunt Sade's place tonight, Pa."

"Well tell Sade, then. You can be thankful, Brother Mott, that you haven't got two wives." Then, his voice taking on the accustomed note of counsel, he adds, "You ought to have one, though. That girl of yours needs a mother, some good woman who can teach her ladylike ways." And the voice goes on, over the sound of hooves, extolling the virtues of one widow or another until the horsemen are lost to sight in their own dust.

When the posse returns the next day, Ezra Mott is riding double by turns on the other men's horses. They had reached Buckhorn Draw at dusk, just as another posse was riding in from Castle Dale. In the dark gorge, each party mistook the other for the outlaws, and before the error was straightened out Ezra Mott's little mare had a bullet in her side. They say that he was furious. His complaints that he had lost three horses in a cause that was none of his damned never-mind anyhow were mingled with Bishop Hardy's impromptu sermon on the duties of law-abiding citizens as the men trailed their dust back into town.

It turned out that Ezra Mott's losses were not as great as he had claimed. The horses the outlaws had taken turned up in his pasture again a few weeks later, giving substance to a suspicion that he had known all along who his winter visitors were and had not been eager to capture them.

Thus the excitement ended, but its echoes continued to reverberate for many years. Even into my own time, the Poplarhaven boys played Robbers' Roost Gang, riding their horses on imaginary raids through every hollow in the dry hills. Stories persisted that the gold was still hidden somewhere in the desert, and we used to make elaborate plans on winter nights for expeditions to recover the treasure as soon as the weather broke in the spring. Grandma said that the town girls were flattered to think that they had danced with famous outlaws at the church socials. The episode raised Retty Mott's stock considerably among the young people, but, as Grandma recalled, she did nothing but moon around all summer and so got little good from it.

Retty Mott at that time was a thin, high-strung girl with suntanned face and arms in a period when fashion dictated creamy white skin. Wild as an unbroken filly, she shocked the good people of Poplarhaven by hitching up her skirts and riding horseback like a man, careless whether her legs were exposed clear to the knee. She had been named Lauretta by the mother she could not have remembered, and she hated to be called Retty. Grandma used to mimic for me the toss of her head and the tone of her voice as she said, "My name is Lau-*ret*-ta." But still Grandma remembered her as an attractive girl and a graceful dancer in the days when she danced with Butch Cassidy.

Shortly after the turn of the century, the high plateau was made a national forest, grazing limits were established, and the day of the open range was over. The large herds were sold off or moved out of the valley. Ezra Mott remained, however. He built a small clapboard house in town and began riding out to work his fields as the other farmers did, but he wasn't much of a farmer. Within a few years he had deteriorated into a slouching and unkempt old man whose days were spent in shuffling back and forth from his house to the pool hall. When my father was young, the boys used to sing a derisory song to the tune of the "Chisholm Trail":

> Ezry Mott stands on the street.
> Tobacco juice dripping clear down to his feet.
> Come a ty-yi-yippy-yippy-yay, yippy-yay.

Retty Mott, at seventeen, ran away with a traveling salesman from Salt Lake. Later, the story goes, she had another husband and lived in Denver. When she returned to Poplarhaven, she brought a little boy with her, but soon a lawman from Colorado came and took him away. It seems he was not her child but her husband's. Retty Mott spent several weeks in the old jail on the town square, where my father and his friends used to climb on one another's shoulders to peek at her through the high, barred windows. I guess that was the start of teasing Retty Mott. When old Ezra Mott finally died, she lived on alone in the little house under the locust trees, always an outsider, lacking the dignity of a widow or the pathos of an old maid, and thus having, as we saw it, no claim upon our sympathies. Each new generation of town boys had a turn at teasing Retty Mott, and year by year the stories of past exploits grew: the giant firecracker dropped down her chimney to explode inside the stovepipe and fill the house with soot; the outhouse overturned on Halloween with Retty Mott inside it; the clothesline rope strung across the doorway to trip her up as she came rushing out of the house.

More puzzling to me than the thoughtless cruelty of the harassment is the realization that none of the romance that surrounded the legends of Butch Cassidy and the great payroll robbery seemed to touch Retty Mott. It is only in recent years that I have come to think of her as a link to that lost time.

One day she hailed me as I was walking past her house and had me come in to help her move a sofa.

"You-ou, You-ou, Boy!" she called in her high-pitched voice, and I felt the tremor of panic that ran through me from earliest childhood whenever she appeared unexpectedly.

That is the only time I was ever inside her house. To my surprise I found it quite cozy and neat. There were cabinets full of books in the front room, and on top of one of the cabinets a photograph of a young boy and another of an attractive girl of about sixteen with a big satin bow on her blouse and a mass of dark hair piled high on her head in the fashion of the 1890s.

The old Relief Society Hall where they held the church socials had fallen into disuse by the time I came along, but it still had the old dance floor, and the two big coal stoves, and the stage at one end where the Poplarhaven Dramatic Club had put on their amateur theatricals. The old folks used to sit near the stoves and watch the young people move around the floor. Bishop Hardy was always present, with a wife on each side of him, frowning at the dancers. He could never quite accept the change from square dancing to couple dancing and would sometimes go out on the floor to separate couples who showed too strong a preference for each other.

When I try to envision the scene at the socials of 1897, it comes to me slowly, filling the old hall with forms and faces that are half familiar, and I can't be sure whether I am making it up or remembering things my grandmother told me. I can see the awkward boys and the unasked girls standing on opposite sides of the floor. The dancers move in a slow circle to the music of the fiddles and a pedal organ. The face of Butch Cassidy emerges from the crowd, the rather pudgy face of the souvenir posters, and I can see that he is dancing with the girl in the photograph at Retty Mott's house. Her slim legs move rapidly and with surprising grace beneath the long skirts, and a strand of dark hair has come loose and swings across her face as she pivots.

The last time I went teasing Retty Mott she burst out of the house at our first shout, before we expected her, scattering us more widely than usual. I found myself in the middle of the next block with Ernie Broadbent, and after catching our breath we began slowly to make our way back, less, I think, to assail the house again than to find our comrades. We were still fifty yards from the house when something rose up from the roadside ditch. We were too startled at first to move, and could only watch as the figure unfolded itself, tall, angular in the darkness, wearing a long, loose robe. She had something heavy in her hand, but she made no motion with it as she spoke, not loud or hysterical but in an appalling undertone.

"Someday," she said, "I'm going to kill me a little Mormon."

TWENTY

The Ward Teacher

On the first Sunday after my fourteenth birthday, I was given the responsibility to watch over the church and see that all the members did their duty, and also to prevent iniquity, hardness with each other, lying, backbiting, and evil speaking. It was a big assignment. Fortunately, I was not alone. All the other boys in town were also ordained teachers at fourteen. And even as deacons for the previous two years we had had a duty to warn, expound, exhort, and teach, besides passing the sacrament each Sunday. These responsibilities had been more theoretical than actual, though, and I would hardly have ventured to warn the patrons of Klecker's pool hall or to expound the gospel to Ed Brinkerhoff, who drove the school bus from Lawrence on weekdays but delivered lengthy scriptural discourses on High Council Sundays. Most of the watching over the church was done by Bishop Brasher and his counselors, so in practice the main duty of my new calling was to make a round of ward teaching visits once a month.

Even so, I didn't take my ordination lightly. When my father and the bishop and Uncle Ray McCandless and Brother McElprang laid their heavy hands on my head, it was as though the weight of manhood were settling on me. Afterwards, they all shook my hand solemnly. Brother McElprang said that I might be envied by a king, and the bishop pointed out that Joseph Smith had been just about my age when he received his first vision. I said little, only nodded my head to show that I was paying attention, but I had already been thinking of those things. I knew that I hadn't taken my religion seriously enough in the past. On several occasions I had gone to the picture show on Sunday nights, and I had often used language and entertained thoughts that were not right for a bearer of the priesthood. Now that I was a teacher, I was determined to do better, to live a more exemplary life.

Shortly after my ordination, Bishop Brasher gave me my ward teaching assignment. I was to accompany Brother Rasmussen on his beat, which would be a great opportunity for me, the bishop said, because he really knew the scriptures. Brother Rasmussen was an elderly man, rather unsteady on his feet but with a stern glare in his eyes and a strong, high-pitched voice. He was one of those who stood up every Fast Sunday to bear their testimonies, and in priesthood meeting when the bishop asked if there were any further business to discuss before we separated into quorums he regularly volunteered advice on the operation of the welfare farm and other ward affairs. The bishop said that I must always respect Brother Rasmussen and follow his direction because he was a high priest and I was only a teacher. But even though I was the junior companion, he added, I had the responsibility to see that the ward teaching was faithfully done and that no offense was given to the people we visited.

I didn't have to worry about making our visits regularly. Brother Rasmussen was as dependable as the dry wind that blew through the valley. On the last Sunday of the month he was always waiting for me at the meetinghouse door, stiff and sour, ready to go. We covered our beat in the same order every month, beginning with the Meeker brothers, who lived on Main Street in the box-like brick house where they had grown up. They belonged to the fairly numerous class in our town known as old batches. Like old maids—another sizeable class— bachelors were always called old, as though senescence were the invariable accompaniment of the single state. But while most of the old maids lived respectable, church-going lives, the old batches tended to be somewhat disreputable. For example, there was Charlie Graham, the window-peeper, periodically captured by some irate husband or father and shipped off to the state hospital for six months, only to reappear and repeat the same cycle again. Or there was Jack Horrocks, who chased young girls when he was drunk. He used to hide behind a tree in the park or in the shadows by the schoolhouse and suddenly lurch out at passing girls with a throaty growl that struck terror into the adolescent female soul. He only engaged in this sport when he was too drunk to run very fast, so he never caught anybody, but he probably still inhabits the nightmares of many women. Kimball Bolden, on the other hand, who was always drunk, never chased anybody, but squinted at one and all through bloodshot eyes while muttering indistinguishable imprecations under his breath.

Ralph and Homer Meeker were fairly respectable, as old batches went. They didn't attend church, but they were hardworking and self-sustaining with a farm and some livestock, and while they usually spent their evenings at Klecker's they seemed to make their way back home again in a not-to-badly-impaired condition. Their dooryard had once been planted with lawn and shrubs, but the grass had gone unmowed for many years and the lilacs and honeysuckle and yellow roses had grown wild, forming a thicket that almost hid the house. The front entrance was entirely overgrown, and to make our visit we had to go around to the kitchen door. The kitchen appeared to be the only room the Meeker brothers occupied, and if it had not been for the smoke coming out of the chimney we might have thought the house was abandoned.

It was always Ralph who opened the door and Homer who cleared off a couple of straight-backed chairs for us to sit on. The brothers looked the same age, but I knew that Ralph was the elder because he always drove the green pickup truck when they went out to the field and Homer had to get out to open and shut the gates. Except for their daily trips to work and the evening excursions to Klecker's, the Meekers seemed to go nowhere, and I envisioned them sitting month after month in that kitchen, staring at the worn linoleum in a silence broken only by the visit of the ward teachers. Brother Rasmussen and I sat stiffly upright in our suits and white shirts while Homer slumped at the table and Ralph tilted his chair back against the hot water tank, both wearing their daily uniform of blue denim overalls and work shoes with flakes of dried manure on the edges.

Brother Rasmussen always had me say the prayer. I got to my feet self-consciously, folded my arms, squinted my eyes shut, and mumbled a few phrases, then sat awkwardly down again. Brother Rasmussen said an emphatic "Amen" and raised his head. Ralph and Homer remained as they were. Then Brother Rasmussen opened his Book of Mormon and read several verses selected, apparently, at random, pausing periodically to clear his throat or blow his nose on a handkerchief that he fished out of the side pocket of his coat. When he had finished reading, he shut the book and looked solemnly from one brother to the other.

"Well, Brethren," he would say, "I didn't see you at Meeting today."

Each time there was a pause while Ralph Meeker shifted his weight on the tilted chair. "Well, no," he drawled, "we don't get out much."

Brother Rasmussen twisted his thin lips. "The Lord has instructed us," he said, "that it is expedient that we meet together often and partake of the sacrament."

Ralph Meeker leaned to one side and spat into the coal scuttle. "We don't get out much," he said.

From the Meeker place it was four blocks to Sister Woodruff's house along a route that was part of my daily walk to and from school. Every step of the way is so deeply impressed on my memory that I can still feel the gravel under my shoes, hear the humming of Oliver Roper's bees, smell the fragrance of the big crabapple at the corner of Dave Leonard's lot, and taste the wild plums that grew near old Sister Allen's place. But on ward teaching day there was no leisure for sensory indulgence. Brother Rasmussen drove an ancient Nash whose engine he raced savagely, whose steering wheel he gripped as though it might try to get away from him, and whose first gear he could never find. Though he threw the lever violently back and forth before giving it a decisive downward tug, he invariably started out in high, the car lurching and gasping until he rammed it into second. Once we got under way things went somewhat better, since there was little traffic on the streets, though we did run Angus Burnside into the ditch one Sunday. Stopping was easy. Brother Rasmussen simply stood on the brake until the engine died.

Sister Woodruff was an elderly widow of imposing frame who lived alone and kept up her house and yard by herself. Her impatience with dust on the sideboard or weeds amid the peonies extended also, I sensed, to the ward teachers who intruded upon her routine every month. There was always a long wait after we knocked and a shifting of the curtains at the window before the door was finally opened. Then she stood blocking the entry for several moments before she spoke.

"It's you again, is it?" she would say. "Wipe your feet before you come in."

Brother Rasmussen always marched in without wiping, but I conscientiously scrubbed my shoes on the rug while Sister Woodruff waved her arms to keep the flies from coming through the open screen door. If one got past her, she sent me an accusing look before she withdrew to her rocking chair and took up her crocheting. We sat on a sofa whose real fabric I never saw, covered as it was by a huge throw.

"Go on, then," Sister Woodruff said. "Go on." But if Brother Rasmussen spent too much time on his reading from the Book of Mormon, she would break in impatiently. "Oh Lard, Ole, get to the point!"

At this, Brother Rasmussen would draw himself up very straight, shut the book emphatically, and speak in an aggrieved tone. "We have come as the representatives of the bishop, Sister Louisa, to bring a scriptural message into your home and to see that there is harmony within the ward and kingdom."

"Oh Lard, Ole," she would say.

The last stop on our ward teaching beat was several thinly settled blocks to the south, through a saltgrass swale. Billy Evans, a gnome-like little man with huge features, threw open the door before we were well out of the car and stood waiting for us, his head bobbing up and down as though it were suspended on a spring.

"The block teachers is here, Martha," he would say to his wife, who was blind and sat always in the same chair, her face turned expectantly toward the sound, her eyelids red and sunken, her toothless gums issuing forth inarticulate cries of greeting. The obvious pleasure that our visit gave the Evanses was a great relief after the indifference or hostility at the other houses, and this was the one part of our ward teaching assignment that I really enjoyed. Billy Evans listened to the scripture reading without interruption, his head bobbing all the while, but the moment Brother Rasmussen closed the book Billy Evans sent forth a torrent of talk, story after story, all having to do with remarkable experiences. He told of visits by the Three Nephites, miraculous accounts of the temple garments protecting those who wore them, tales of enemies of the church being smitten. I found his stories fascinating, but Brother Rasmussen didn't like them at all. After two or three unsuccessful attempts to break into the stream of talk, he would retreat to a gloomy silence, his lips twisting tighter and tighter until at last he lurched to his feet and declared that a ward teaching visit should not be unduly prolonged.

Except for the good feeling I brought away from the Evans home each month, I couldn't see that ward teaching was contributing much to my program for spiritual improvement. I had cut out Sunday picture shows and started attending Mutual every Tuesday night, even when they didn't have activities, but these were only external things. I knew that the real growth had to happen inside, and I was finding that perfecting my life was a bigger job than I had anticipated. I had always prayed more or less regularly at bedtime, uttering thanks for my many blessings and asking for the things I wanted, or thought I ought to want, but I became aware that I was only speaking rote phrases into the darkness. When a visiting apostle said in stake conference that the spirit is most receptive during the early morning hours, I began setting my alarm for 5:00 A.M. so that I could study the scriptures and pray before breakfast, but I found that my spirit was most receptive to sleep at that hour. Almost every morning I would doze off in the middle of a sentence and wake up to find that I couldn't remember anything I had read. When the bishop told us in priesthood meeting about Enos and how he had gone to the forest and prayed all day and night until he received an answer from the Lord, I made up my mind to follow his example. The next Saturday I arose early and went fasting to the willow thicket by the Big Canal, intending to pray all day. I found a secluded spot and knelt down, but after just a few minutes my knees started to hurt and I ran out of things to say. I stayed there for a while with my eyes shut, hoping that something more would come, but instead I became conscious of the natural sounds around me, little rustlings in the weeds and the plop of a water rat into the canal, and I realized that I wasn't thinking about spiritual things at all. After another attempt or two to get in tune, I gave it up and went home, arriving in time for breakfast. I was beginning to suspect that I might not have been a valiant spirit in the pre-existence.

Still, I didn't want to give up. Surely there must be some spiritual experience in store for me if only I would prepare myself for it. Sometimes, lying in my bed in the dark, I would try to imagine what it must have been like for Joseph Smith, how it would be to have some evil power assail you when you tried to pray. The thought of it sent a tremor of fear through me. Yet it was equally frightening to think of angelic visitations. What if, right at that very moment, a light should appear in my bedroom and begin to grow until it was above the brightness of midday? Sometimes I worked myself into such a fright that I buried my head under the covers, with only my nose sticking out for air, and slept that way all night.

On one ward teaching visit, Brother Rasmussen tried to persuade the Meeker brothers that they ought to get married, pointing out to them that every bearer of the priesthood had an obligation to raise up a righteous posterity. "Now you have the means to support a wife, a good house and all of that," he said, looking around the cluttered kitchen. "You could use a woman's touch here, curtains on the windows and the like of that." Then he proceeded to enumerate the widows and old maids in town.

Ralph Meeker showed his yellow teeth. "Naw," he said, "we ain't int'rested in none of your widahs."

When Brother Rasmussen mentioned Lula Brown as an eligible maiden lady, Ralph Meeker snorted contemptuously.

"Hell, there ain't enough juice in her to drownd a pissant."

Brother Rasmussen grew indignant at this and declared that any man who denied a woman her chance to be a mother in Israel would be held accountable at the last day. Ralph Meeker, silent again, grinned with his yellow teeth.

During the summer months we usually found Sister Woodruff working in her yard, wearing an everyday housedress and a wide-brimmed straw hat. Brother Rasmussen would twist his lips at this open violation of the Sabbath, and Sister Woodruff, in turn, showed irritation at being interrupted at her gardening.

"Sunday work will never prosper," he announced one sweltering afternoon. Sister Woodruff, who had been loosening the soil around her rosebushes, stood up with her face aflame.

"Maybe you should try working on Sundays, Ole," she said when she had caught her breath. "That would be *one* day, at least."

I sensed that these were the occasions the bishop had in mind when he had cautioned me to be sure no offense was given, but I didn't see what I could do. I felt that Brother Rasmussen was not as tactful and long-suffering as he might have been. On the other hand, though, Sister Woodruff seemed a little deficient in respect for the priesthood. I tried to think of some way to suggest to them that they were treating each other with some degree of hardness, but Brother Rasmussen always beat me to it.

"Sister Louisa," he said sternly one day, "the Lord is displeased with those who mock the priesthood."

This time Sister Woodruff didn't even look up from her work. "Priesthood indeed!" she said. "You were a fool before you had the priesthood, Ole. All the priesthood has done is make you a pompous fool."

When school started in the fall, I began to take seminary from Brother Fowles, who had just arrived in town. He gave a new impetus to my determination to become a more spiritual person. He was obviously a very spiritual man himself. He came from Salt Lake and knew many of the general authorities of the church personally and could tell numerous stories about the spiritual experiences in their lives. Of course, the spirituality didn't come just from living in Salt Lake. Brother Fowles also had many stories that showed what a wicked city it was, stories which confirmed my impressions drawn from the odor of cigar smoke in the lobby of the Moxum Hotel and from Ferd Nichols's girl cousins, who had tried to teach us to do the dirty boogie.

We were supposed to be studying the Old Testament in seminary, but Brother Fowles didn't limit himself just to the text. When he read Genesis, he told us that Cain was still wandering the earth because of his sin in killing his brother and entering into a secret combination with Satan. Cain was a great big black man, Brother Fowles said, bigger than any ordinary man because he came from before the Flood. He told about people who had met Cain, and how he begged them to kill him because he couldn't die. I was nervous about going out at dusk after hearing these stories because it was always when people were alone at dusk that they met Cain.

Brother Fowles also told us about Ouija Boards, which I had never seen except in the Gympy Ward Christmas catalog. Evidently they were very common in Salt Lake and very dangerous because if you played them you were tampering with spiritual powers and could easily fall into the hands of the devil. Brother Fowles told us about one group of kids who were members of the church and went to seminary but nevertheless began to experiment with Ouija Boards. When they asked the Ouija whether the church was true, the pointer flew off the board and hit the wall, and later the girl whose house they played in saw a dark presence in a corner of the room and they couldn't get rid of it until the bishop came and blessed the house. Another time, some boys were working the Ouija Board in the cemetery, and one of them became possessed and tried to kill himself, and the others had to haul him forcibly to the bishop for a blessing.

I devoured Brother Fowles's teachings eagerly in seminary, but when I thought about them later, especially when I was alone at night, they made me uneasy. I would certainly not do the things those kids had done. I had no desire to approach the spirits through the Ouija Board, or to get a testimony of the devil by praying to him, as a foolish missionary had done and a huge man on a black horse had ridden right into his room and carried him off before the eyes of his companion. But if it was dangerous to tamper with spiritual powers, it was equally destructive, Brother Fowles said, to live without the spirit. I didn't want to turn out like Ralph and Homer Meeker, totally insensitive to spiritual things. Nor did I want to be like some people Brother Fowles had known, who tried to intellectualize the gospel and who were consequently led astray by the philosophies of men. The worst thing of all, he said, was to have an intellectual testimony, to try to understand the things of God through human reason instead of by the pure witness of the spirit.

In this frame of mind, I began to appreciate our visits to the Evanses more and more. For Billy Evans there seemed to be no demarcating line between the physical and spiritual worlds. A man could be working in a coal mine, just going about his regular business, and have a sudden rockfall kill the fellow working next to him and yet leave him unharmed, except for crushing his foot, but that wasn't covered by his temple garments. In Billy Evans I felt that I had found a living example of that humble, simple faith which Brother Fowles recommended. To be sure, he rarely came out to church meetings, and I couldn't remember him ever holding a job in the ward, but that was probably because he needed to stay with his wife.

During our October visit, Billy Evans got going on the Three Nephites and the trail of wonders they left behind them as they journeyed through the world. On one occasion a man he knew had been stranded in the mountains by a snowstorm, and because the wood was wet he couldn't get a fire started and was just about to freeze to death, when suddenly, as he was striking his last match, someone stepped up behind him and threw something like gasoline onto the fire and it flared up instantly. But when the man looked around, nobody was there.

"That was one of the Nephites, sure enough," Billy Evans said, his head bobbing up and down.

I asked him whether he had ever met one of the Three Nephites himself.

He bobbed and grinned mysteriously. "I know some things about them," he said. "I know some things I ain't allowed to tell."

I was tremendously impressed at this because Brother Fowles had told us that some people receive manifestations so special that they cannot be revealed to anyone else.

Brother Rasmussen terminated the visit abruptly, as usual, but when we were in the car he turned to me before starting the engine.

"Young man, the devil will deceive the very elect if he can," he said.

I nodded. I wasn't sure exactly what he meant, but I read in the remark some disapproval of Billy Evans, perhaps because he didn't come to church regularly. However, I was beginning to wonder about Brother Rasmussen. I suspected that he might have an intellectual testimony.

The next month, Brother Rasmussen had the flu and couldn't do his ward teaching. I was going to go with my father, but something came up at the last minute, and I faced the prospect of covering the beat by myself. When I thought of those inhospitable dwellings, I considered not going out at all that month. I could tell the bishop that I had forgotten until it was too late. Or I could even report that I had made the visits. Nobody was likely to tell on me. But as soon as these thoughts entered my mind, my conscience stung me. Here I had been praying that I might become a more faithful servant, yet I was weakening at the first sign of adversity.

The visits turned out better than I expected. It almost seemed as if Ralph and Homer Meeker and Sister Woodruff were glad to see me, though they said no more than usual. At Sister Woodruff's, it occurred to me to offer to come back the next Saturday and fix the loose hinge on her gate. She looked up from her needlework with something like surprise. "That would be very nice," she said.

The late autumn dusk was falling by the time I walked out to Billy Evans's place, but I was rather enjoying my ward teaching now and was in no hurry to finish. I tried to get Billy Evans to tell me more about the Three Nephites, but his thoughts were running along different lines on this night.

"The Nephites isn't the only ones still walking the earth, you know," he said.

"I know. There's Cain too."

"Cain, yes," he said. "And the Gadianton Robbers."

I had read about the Gadianton band in the Book of Mormon, but it had never occurred to me that any evidences of them might still remain.

"They was all through these mountains, up and down," Billy Evans said. "And they're still there." Then he told how in the early days the people had tried to settle a certain place down by St. George but nothing would grow there, and Brigham Young told them it was because it had been a habitation of the Gadianton Robbers.

"And there's just such another spot right up here in the foothills," he said. "You seen it, ain't you, just past Rowleys', where there ain't nothing but little scrubby bushes?"

I tried to visualize the place but could not remember one spot that looked much different from the others. But of course I had not known what to look for. Billy Evans went on to tell of people traveling between towns at night who came upon a crowd of strange figures with pale faces and weird eyes who ran alongside them as they rode and kept pace no matter how fast they drove their horses, dropping back only when they neared a town.

"Matter of fact," he added, "I seen them myself, or as good as seen them." It happened when he was working at a sheep camp as a young man, he said. He had ridden into town for supplies and had hung around the beer joint so long that he had to ride back to camp in the dark.

"Well, when I got up to where the canyon narrows, I begun to hear the sounds," he said. "They was moving along in the trees at the side of the road, only of course I couldn't see nothing in the dark. When I stopped, they stopped, and it was as still as death. When I begun to move again, they begun too. There wasn't no way I could get away. Well, I begun to call on the Lord, you bet. Then, all of a sudden, there come a sound like a bell ringing, way up high, like it come from the rocks. That scared me more than ever cause I thought it was a signal for them to get me, and I begun to call on the Lord more and more. I told him that if he would help me out this here one time, I'd stay clear of beer joints and wouldn't do nothing to offend him. And lo and behold"—he paused and bobbed his head emphatically—"lo and behold, the clouds parted and a great light broke through. A great light. It was something like the moon, but it wasn't no moon. It didn't shine nowhere else only just round about me and the pony, keeping the Gadiantons off. They followed me all the way to the camp, but they stayed back in the shadows. I was protected, you see, and they daresn't come any closer. Next morning, though, we found four sheep dead and not a mark on them."

When I finally left the house, night had fallen, and a cold wind was blowing from the canyon. I hadn't realized how dark it would be, and I found myself wishing I had started my visits earlier so I could have walked home in the daylight. The mountains loomed black against the last rosy streaks of cloud in the western sky, and involuntarily I thought of the Gadianton Robbers roaming there all through the centuries, on the lookout for somebody who wasn't protected. Northward, toward home, the pale surface of the road descended into the saltgrass swale before it climbed the next rise, where there were houses. I stood still in the road and listened. Perfect silence. Not even the insect sounds of summer nights. And Billy Evans had said that the Gadianton Robbers avoided towns. This was in town, but just barely; the swale drained the west fields, and beyond them there were only the open flats and the mountains.

I started walking at a deliberate pace, in order to hold onto a sense of normality. The sound of my shoes on the gravel seemed to come from the dry weeds at the side of the road. If a car should come by, I thought, I could walk rapidly while its lights illuminated the road and maybe get through the swale to the houses on the other side before it was altogether dark again. But no car came. I realized that I was breathing a fragmentary prayer as I walked. Of course, that was the answer. The Lord would surely protect me while I was engaged in his work, but I had to demonstrate faith. I had to pray properly, vocally, and kneeling. I dropped to my knees at the side of the road, bowed my head, and shut my eyes. But I couldn't keep them shut. They would pop open in the middle of a phrase to see if something was approaching. When I tried to concentrate on keeping my eyes shut, I lost touch with the words I was speaking. Fear seemed to thicken around me, and I was trembling with cold.

Brother Fowles had said that the closer you got to perfection the harder Satan would try to hold you back. That was what had happened to Joseph Smith when he went to the Sacred Grove. But he had cried out for help, and the light had come, the light in the grove, the presences.

I scrambled to my feet. "It's okay," I said aloud. "I'm all right."

My footfalls came back from the dead growth at the sides of the road like an invisible horde keeping pace, breaking into a run when I did and staying precisely even with me. But except for the minute points of the stars against the cold vault, there was no light. Hugging the darkness about me like a cloak, I ran for home.

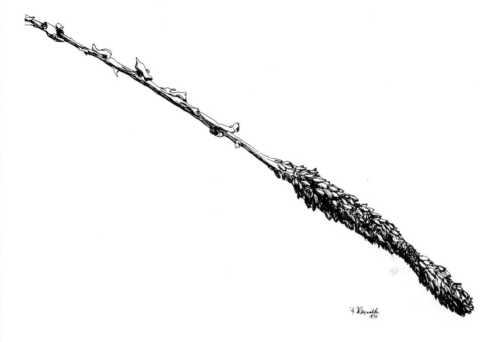

TWENTY-ONE

A Season on the Mountain

"Ah! frère, compagnon, voyageur, comme nous étions persuadés, tous deux, que le bonheur était proche, et qu'il allait suffire de se mettre en chemin pour l'atteindre!"
— *Alain-Fournier*, Le Grand Meaulnes

My father spent his thirteenth summer at a construction camp in the canyon, sleeping and waking in the mountain chill, bathing in the snowmelt stream, walking through shimmering aspen groves, and watching the scraper blade cut through the ageless leaf mold. As he described it in later years, it was the most memorable summer of his life, and from hearing his stories I came to think of it as my season on the mountain too, an elevation from which to survey the lower landscape of existence.

Many of the families who settled Poplarhaven in the 1870s had come from Sanpete Valley, so there were strong traditional ties, but travel from one valley to the other had always been difficult, requiring a hard journey on a wagon track over the high plateau or else a long detour around it. The local people had tried for years to get a better road and finally received approval from the Bureau of Public Roads in 1925, a time, ironically, when the passing of the pioneer generation had brought a loosening of the ties to Sanpete.

The building of the road took two summers. It wasn't much of a road, merely graded dirt with bridges instead of fords across the streams, passable only in dry weather. But it represented the fulfillment of a long-held hope. The project was divided up into small segments that were contracted to local people, not contractors by trade, most of them, but farmers and stockmen who were accustomed to building their own canals, reservoirs, cellars, barns. Grandpa won a contract for half a mile of road and a bridge across the creek, and he took Dad with him as camp tender. They left the valley on the first of June, 1925, at the beginning of the summer heat, Dad sitting beside Grandpa on the lead wagon, packed with tents, tools, food, and sacks of oats for the horses. Behind them, Bert Westover and Silas Cox, the hired men, followed with the other team and wagon, hauling the scraper and a jag of hay. They would have started before dawn— always Grandpa's way—and kept the early morning coolness with them as they went up the canyon. There was already a graded road as far as the Forks, twenty miles from town. I have traveled the route many times by automobile and can imagine the slow ascent of the wagons as they skirted the fields at the canyon mouth, passed the piñon pines and junipers of the foothills, and came under the shadow of Gentry Mountain with its steep cliffs and talus slopes. The long-needle pines begin at Deer Creek and Meetinghouse canyons, and at Bear Canyon the road goes around a big bend where you lose sight of the valley. The cottonwoods along the creek gradually give way to blue spruce between Trail Canyon and Mill Fork, and a mile or so farther on the canyon narrows so that there is barely enough room for the road beside the creek. They would have stopped to water the teams at the Blind Canyon ford and perhaps have eaten their midday meal at Horse Canyon. The sheltered slopes on the left hand were densely forested with fir at that time, forests destroyed by a massive fire in 1939. At the Forks, where the two main branches of the creek join, they followed the right-hand stream for another mile until they reached their campsite, a small side canyon a hundred yards from the creek.

The journey took them from summer to early spring. There were still snowbanks in the shaded spots, and the quaking aspens had the delicate gold-green of their first leaf. Grandpa would have wasted no time in setting up camp, erecting the wall tents on an open flat and building an enclosure of poles against a rock ledge to protect the hay and grain. Dad cooked a supper of fried beef and potatoes on the sheepherder stove that they set up in front of the supply tent, and they would have fallen into bed at dusk, tired from the long day but with everything prepared for the morrow's work.

Sleep comes hard the first night in the mountains. There are unfamiliar sounds, the weight of the heavy camp quilts, the odor of canvas. I imagine Dad lying awake for what seemed a long time, then sleeping but waking again in the dark to hear the creek and the downslope wind and feel the damp night chill penetrate the tent. As he burrowed deeper into the quilts and tried to sleep again, he would have become conscious of the rustlings, scrapings, scratchings of the nocturnal life in the preternatural darkness just beyond the canvas walls. There is a moment in such a night when one senses the blind power of the wilderness, the zero in the bone, and regrets having left the familiar human world. The feeling of isolation is only slightly mitigated by the snores of the sleeping men or the occasional snort and stamp of the horses, hobbled and turned out to graze farther up the canyon. Just when he had come to feel that he would never sleep, he slept and woke at first light to the smell of woodsmoke and the clatter of pans outside the tent.

He threw off the covers quickly, so that he wouldn't have time to shrink from the cold, and pulled on his stiff clothes, going outside to tie his shoes by the stove. Before he had a chance to get warm, Grandpa sent him to the spring for a bucket of water, and he walked up through the clearing, leaving footprints in the frost that had settled on the grass during the night. The spring was free of ice where it emerged from a limestone bank, but a thin glaze covered the stream a few yards below. He broke off a piece the size of a plate and held it up to his eyes to view a twisted landscape of white and green. He dropped the ice and it shattered at his feet. The air came into his lungs as though it were the first breath ever drawn, and he plunged the brass bucket into the clear pool and brought it forth dripping. A thick mist had settled in the bottom of the main canyon, and from where he stood he could look across its undulating white surface to the forested slope on the other side, still in shadow except for the topmost ridge, where the sun illuminated a huge, half-dead Douglas fir. As he walked back to the camp, he saw a form emerging from the mist like an apparition. It was Bert Westover, coming up from the creek carrying trout for their breakfast.

When I was eight or ten years old, the Forest Service opened up the little side canyon for cabin lots, and Dad obtained a lease on the lot nearest the spring. On summer weekends we would drive up there for picnics and spend the afternoon measuring and planning. Dad would explain how the cabin would be arranged and how, after it was built, we could stay for a week, two weeks at a time, maybe even an entire summer. He disliked the cabins that were erected on other lots, feeling that they didn't harmonize with the setting. Really he would have preferred to have the little canyon all to himself. He could never afford to build the cabin he planned, and eventually he surrendered the lease and as far as I know did not revisit the site during the last ten years of his life.

The days soon settled into a routine at the camp. Grandpa got up first and made the fire and cooked breakfast. Bert Westover disappeared into the mist that hung over the creek, while Silas Cox slung the tie ropes over his shoulder and walked up the canyon to where the teams had been left to graze. The horses had their morning scoop of oats while the men ate breakfast, usually fresh-caught trout with bacon and eggs and canned beans. Some mornings, when he got up early enough, Dad followed Bert down to the creek. Bert Westover fished without hook or line, crouching on the bank like a small bear, gazing intently at the water as if contemplating his own reflection, but really looking past it at the underwater forms. He could remain motionless for a long time; then suddenly with a single swift movement his hand darted into the water and emerged with a fish struggling in its grasp.

I never saw Bert Westover catch fish, but I can remember watching Uncle Lindon, my mother's elder brother, for years a sheepherder. He too seemed slow, unhurried, but there is a quickness that is a gift. I trained myself to see into the water and make out the fish holding its position against the current with a seemingly effortless motion of tail and fins. But I never even came close to catching one.

Even before my hand touched the water, the fish would give a sudden flick and simply disappear, leaving me to grasp the icy water where it had been. It was as though it had read a signal from my brain.

After breakfast, Dad was left to wash the dishes and clean up the camp while the men harnessed the teams and began the day's work. The contract involved clearing some trees from the right-of-way, cutting off the point of a hill, and filling in some low ground, besides building a bridge across the creek. (Earlier in the spring, Grandpa had dug up several small spruces from the right-of-way and planted them in his yard in town. By my time they had become landmark trees, blue-green pyramids fifty feet tall.) The cut required some blasting, which Bert Westover handled, as he had worked in the mines. The dirt was moved with a horse-drawn scraper, smaller than the better-known Fresno scraper but similar in design. The scraper was shaped like a large scoop shovel, about four feet wide and perhaps two-and-a-half deep, made of hardwood reinforced with iron, with a steel blade at the front. The scoop was attached at each side to a yoke in such a way that it could pivot forward and back. The yoke in turn was fastened to the double tree and the tongue that ran between the horses. The operator walked behind the scraper and controlled the scoop by means of a straight wooden handle that extended from its rear, while the teamster walked to one side holding the reins. When they reached the place from which the dirt was to be taken, the operator guided the scoop blade into the earth at just the right angle: too shallow an angle and it merely slid along the ground, picking up nothing; too steep and it would either bury itself in the ground or else flip over. When full, the scoop was dragged along the ground to the place where it was to be dumped. Then the operator thrust the handle forward to dump the load. In this position, the blade acted as a grader, smoothing out the dirt.

Slowly, pass by pass, they moved earth for the roadbed in this way. We still used the scraper occasionally for small jobs when I was a boy. It could hold perhaps three or four cubic feet of dirt, and I remember how painfully slow it seemed in moving any appreciable quantity of materials. Yet in 1906 Grandpa had worked with the crew that built the reservoir on top of the plateau, and the dam they constructed is still in place: probably two hundred yards long and thirty feet high, thousands upon thousands of cubic yards of earth, tens of thousands of passes with team and scraper.

Most of the construction work was too heavy for a boy, and so in addition to cooking the noon and evening meals Dad ran errands, found his own little projects to do, or simply watched. He spent a couple of days building a catch system for the waters of a small spring that seeped from a bank, channeling it to a spout that the men could drink from. While Grandpa and Silas Cox ran the scraper, Dad helped Bert Westover with the other team drag timbers to the site of the bridge. Bert was a skilled woodsman, apparently unhurried, yet his ax bit rapidly and precisely through the wood sending honey-colored chips flying out in a steady stream. On one occasion, Dad was standing at what he thought was a safe distance to watch the felling of an unusually large tree. As the cut neared completion, Bert paused and called him to come nearer and stand a few yards to one side. Then he finished with a flurry of strokes that brought the tree down, twisting as it fell and landing right on the spot where Dad had originally been standing.

The men did not work on Sundays. Every two weeks, Grandpa hitched a team to the light wagon and drove down to the Forks where he met Grandma, who had brought supplies in the Dodge. One Sunday Dad and Grandpa rode up the canyon. As they came to other construction sites, they paused to talk with the men and measure the progress of the work. In its upper reaches the canyon grew wider, with broad water meadows and rolling slopes. Near the summit, it became a lush valley where some Sanpete people had a summer dairy. The cows fed in the cool meadows, and the dairyman's wife and daughters made butter and cheese which they carried down to Sanpete Valley for sale. Grandpa bought a supply of butter and a wooden tub of cottage cheese, and on the way back to camp he purchased a freshly butchered lamb from a sheepherder who was camped on the sagebrush flat below Eccles Canyon.

As the season advanced the days grew hot even in the canyon, the tents stifling and heavy with the odor of tar. But the heat of the day was brief. The sun rose late and went down early behind the canyon walls, and the nights were always chilly. Dad frequently took a walk at nightfall, going up the little canyon or along the creek, drinking in the fragrant air and listening to the woodland noises that now seemed to have nothing alien in them. If he was walking by the creek, he might hear the splash of a beaver and see the sleek head moving at the point of a wedge of water. In the mornings he routinely took the brass bucket up to the ridge, which always caught the first rays of the sun.

One Sunday he made up his mind to hike up to the tree. He started right after breakfast, climbing the slope above Pole Canyon which was covered with mixed groves of fir and aspen interspersed with patches of sagebrush. The mountainside was steeper than he had thought, and the climb much longer. Each time he came out of the trees, he looked back to the camp to measure his progress. It came to seem very far away, much farther than the top of the ridge had appeared, but when he looked upward there was still a long slope ahead. Because of the angle of the incline, he had lost sight of the big tree and could see only a rounded horizon that continued to recede before him as he climbed. He began to wish that he had brought some water along. Breathing through his mouth in an effort to meet the demands of his burning lungs, he felt his throat go dry and his tongue fuzzy. Still he labored on, and eventually the slope grew less steep, rounding toward the top. Then he caught sight of the tree again, some distance off to the left instead of straight ahead, so he had deflected his course without realizing it.

It was indeed a huge fir for our region, more than six feet in diameter at its base with a crown eighty feet high. The lower half was dead, with dry skeletal limbs, but it was still green at the top. Dad found that it did not actually stand on the crest of the ridge as it appeared to do from camp, but that there were a few more yards to climb before he could see what lay on the other side. From the crest he looked down on a densely wooded slope then up to another ridge and yet another, higher ridge beyond. Looking back toward the main canyon, he found that he could see beyond the mountain that lay behind the camp and into the Left Fork. Down-canyon there was shape and form, the water-carved trough that gathered tributaries from the high plateau, but in every other direction the plateau seemed to go on forever in a maze of ridges and hollows. The vastness of the landscape, empty of human life (for the camp could not be seen from this point) suddenly assailed him, and he felt a rush of panic such as he had experienced on the first night, a sensation of his own smallness and weakness, of isolation, a feeling that he had intruded on alien ground. Though the sun was almost overhead now and the day growing hot, he shivered a little and began to make his way back to camp.

He did not go back down the face of the slope but worked his way into a little ravine that led into Pole Canyon. From above it appeared to be only a small notch in the mountainside, but as he descended he found that it was deeper than he had thought and more sheltered. He followed a dry streambed through the aspen shade until he came upon a spring that fed a pool below a large rock. He lay on his stomach and drank from the pool, not dipping the water in his hand as his father did but touching his lips to the surface and drawing it straight in, cold and sweet. He drank deep, paused, and drank again, then settled on a flat rock with his back against an aspen trunk. The panic was gone now, though he was no less alone. But there was nothing troubling in this isolation. There was comfort in the smell of the damp moss, the sound of the trickling stream as it flowed from the pool, the rattling of the aspen leaves in the slightest breeze. He remained there for a long time, how long he did not know, basking in peace and security. When he finally got to his feet to go on, he was suddenly flooded with a sensation of blessedness such as he had never experienced before. Then he noticed for the first time that something had been carved in the bark of the tree he had been leaning against, the initials A. M. H. and the date 1887. The cut had made a black spreading scar on the smooth white aspen bark, but he saw it not as a desecration of the wilderness but a testament that one other person, at least, had been in the same place and perhaps felt the same sensations. Pulling his hunting knife from its scabbard on his belt, he carefully cut his own initials and the date below the others. The clean new cuts showed green through the paper-smooth bark.

Dad read a good deal as a boy, and in fact he had brought a supply of books with him for the summer on the mountain. After he had cleaned up the lunch things, he sometimes retired to the stuffy tent and lay on his bedroll and read for two or three hours. From the books that remained in my grandparents' house when I came along, and from the titles listed in the diary that Dad kept a year or so later, I gather that his reading fare was standard boys' adventure stories, with *The Count of Monte Cristo* the most "literary" title, the same book that James Joyce portrays as having colored Stephen Dedalus's romantic imagination a generation earlier.

A young schoolteacher had come to Poplarhaven the previous year, evidently a woman of considerable intelligence. She stayed only one year, but she took a special liking to Dad and later sent him a case of muskmelons from her new home. I wonder if she might also have introduced him to books that were unlikely at that time and place, books, perhaps such as I improbably discovered in my adolescence. If he

had read Alain-Fournier's little novel about provincial French school-
boys in their quest for a mysterious lost domain, would it have colored his response to the woods and mountains? Would he, as I did,
have explored the canyons half in hope of coming upon the decayed
chateau with its beautiful and doomed chatelaine? But in the books
that I know he read there is also the image of the secret place—the
secret garden, the secret path that leads to a realm of perfect freedom
and fulfillment, a lost domain of pure presence. Only Alain-Fournier
stands somewhat apart in representing the powerful yet etherealized
eroticism of the adolescent dream, and in intimating that the lost domain is death.

They finished the contracted work by the middle of August and
returned to the valley, but there was one last renewal of the season on
the mountain that came the following year. In August 1926 a celebration was held to mark the completion of the road. Crowds of people
from both valleys came for the three-day encampment, their tents
filling the grove above Boulger Creek and spilling out onto the flats.
Each day there were band concerts, baseball games, boxing and
wrestling matches, horse races and pulling contests, and in the evenings campfire programs and dances. Even the governor came for one
day.

Dad and his family attended the celebration, of course, amid the
dust and the crowds, a far cry from the isolation of the mountain the
previous summer. He was struck by the beauty and approachability of
the Sanpete girls, which made opportunities even for a shy adolescent
like himself. With his friends and alone, he went visiting among the
camps, found girls to hold hands with at the campfire programs, girls
who would stay up late for the dances, exquisite, mysterious girls who
seemed altogether unlike the ones he had grown up with. On the last
day he went hiking with a girl up to the waterfall. He couldn't remember her name or even which Sanpete town she came from, but at
twelve or thirteen she had grace and charm, and it was exciting to
walk with her on the mountains where he had once walked alone.
The sun went down before they got back to the campground, and the
evening chill fell suddenly. She shivered a little in her summer dress,
and with unaccustomed boldness he put his arm around her waist and
drew her unresisting against him. Thus, arm in arm, they walked
down the trail in the fading light, when suddenly, from a grove across
the canyon there came a high-pitched cry. It came again, a voice call-

ing a name, "Chloe! Chloe!" After his initial start, he realized that it was the signal for the beginning of the dance, a male quartet singing a popular song of the season. But the impression remained that the cry had come directly from the forest, as though nature itself had articulated the longing that stirred in his own consciousness. The songs that he composed in later years were, I suspect, efforts to recapture that moment, his own glimpse of the lost domain. The invisible voices continued, chanting the formula of the endless quest:

> Through the black of night,
> I've got to go where you are. . . .

The campground was stirring as they approached, and the girl decorously detached herself from his grasp. It was the last night of the celebration, the end of the season. Soon the saxophones would begin their reedy wail, and couples would start to move around the improvised wooden dance floor in the dim light of the kerosene lamps. Over in the grove, the quartet was singing the last bars of the song:

> There no chains can bind you,
> If you live, I'll find you. . . .

It occurred to him then that he would never again be as happy as he was at that moment.

TWENTY-TWO

The Farther Field

A row of cottonwoods ran along the lane on the north side of the forty acres, their leaves, in August, a dark green that reflected no light. Earlier in the week, when we were piling, we had eaten our midday meal in their shade. Grandpa, his sleeves rolled above his elbows, forearms scrubbed in the irrigation ditch, had unfolded the table-cloth in the blue enameled dishpan and portioned out roast beef sandwiches and slices of applesauce cake which we washed down with lemonade from mason jars, sweet with rationed sugar.

Now we were hauling. Grandpa and Len Wight pitched on while my cousin Ted and I tromped as the hayrack moved slowly through the hay piles that stretched across the field in ranks and files like troops on parade in the newsreels at the Thursday night picture shows. When we reached the top of the field, Len shambled to the ditch and dunked his head in the water, coming back with drenched features distorted in a wide grin. I felt the sweat burning on my own face as I squinted into the sunlight. To the west, beyond the patches of trees that marked Anton Nielson's field, rose the fortress-like es-carpment of the high plateau, barren except for a few junipers that clung to the steep talus slopes and an irregular row of pines silhou-etted against the sky on the topmost ridge.

This was the farther field, two miles from home, yet still within the secure circle of my first world. More easily than I could retrace my movements of yesterday, I could still locate the exact spots where as-paragus used to grow along the fencelines and where the yellow cur-rant and black currant and bullberry bushes stood. Though it has been forty years since I last walked it, I can follow in my mind virtu-ally step by step the path that led up the wash to the alkaline pool where we used to catch suckers and minnows in the intervals of field work.

While the places remain indelibly impressed on my memory, particular occasions tend to blur and fade. But I do recall one August day when we were hauling the last of the second cutting. We were a scanty crew, really just Grandpa and Len and Ted. I was a mere hanger-on, too small to pitch, too light to tromp. Uncle Merlin was working the day shift at Hiawatha, and Dad had a summer job as a bookkeeper at Horse Canyon. Len Wight, who was 4-F because of his deafness, was one of the few field hands available, and we were no doubt fortunate to have him that day though I might not have thought so at the time. Len troubled me. He spoke in nasal tones that I found incomprehensible, and I had early adopted the practice of simply nodding agreement to everything he said. Perhaps because of his difficulty in verbal communication, he had developed a set of exaggerated physical gestures. He was largely free of these movements while he was working, but whenever he paused he would twist his torso from side to side and stretch his neck forward while he curled his lips back to show his teeth like a horse, not with a spastic motion but rather a strained, frustrated violence, as though some force were swelling inside him. With children his body language took more aggressive forms, with sharp jabs in the ribs from his forefinger or mock assaults with the pitchfork. I had been afraid of him when I was younger, and I still was, a little, though I had learned not to show it.

When we hauled the farther field, Grandpa made the loads even bigger than usual because each one had to be taken to the haystack at the first field or all the way in to the barn, and it was difficult to complete more than six or seven trips in a day. I loved those long hauls on the gently swaying hayrack. I remember one trip when Ted reached out and tore a branch from a bullberry bush as we brushed by. Then he and I nibbled at the puckery fruit while Len made sour faces at us from his nest in the hay. For the first mile, our route ran along narrow farm lanes. When we reached the southern boundary of town, the road widened and went up a hill where the horses had to strain against their harnesses. Here we passed the first field, with its haystack already rounded off to shed the winter storms, and drove on for another mile with the town on our right and fields on the left.

After unloading the hay in the barn, we rested on the shady lawn for a few minutes while Grandpa went inside to listen to the war news on the radio. When he returned, we climbed aboard the hayrack again for the jolting ride back out to the field. As we passed the old Marshall place, we heard shouts and saw a gang of boys playing combat games with rubber guns in the empty barn. If we hadn't been working in the hay, Ted and I would have been there with them, stalking one another, waiting in ambush to jump out suddenly and pull the clothespin trigger that shot a strip of rubber. If you were hit, you were dead and had to lie still and count to one hundred before you could join in the game again. It wasn't easy to find the prewar innertubes from which to cut strips of rubber for ammunition. Synthetic rubber was no good.

The war lies behind my early memories as a constant but half-unreal backdrop. To me it meant ration coupons, and a scarcity of chewing gum, and comic books wherein Marines slaughtered fiendish but myopic Japanese on South Pacific islands. I remember the stars in the windows and the young men home on furlough hanging around the drugstore in their sailor suits, and when we went over to Castle Dale to visit Grandma Ungerman on Sunday afternoons we listened to the letters that came from Uncle Lorin, who was in Italy and had "seen action," whatever that meant. Occasionally an airplane flew over our valley, rarely enough that we would run outside to look at it. Some of my classmates collected cards from cereal boxes that showed the different models of military aircraft, and they would engage in loud playground arguments as to whether the distant speck in the sky was a P-38 or a P-61. The newspapers carried caricatures of a Hitler and Mussolini and Tojo who seemed so remote from our own human standard as to be almost figures of fantasy, scarcely more real than the villainous Black Pete in the Mickey Mouse books. The war was very far away, far beyond the guardian barrier of the mountains which surrounded "the peaceful vales of Deseret," as the song we sang in church put it.

Of the several men from our valley who lost their lives in the war, I can remember only Pete Grange. Audrey Sandberg was the Red Cross respresentative in Poplarhaven, and when word came that he had been wounded on Okinawa she asked my mother to help break the news to his family. I remember the sound of the phrase, "wounded in action," and the sudden grief of Pete's sister, who was working at the Post Office. The Granges lived on the other side of town, but we knew them as we knew all of the families in Poplarhaven. Pete had been one of my father's students at the high school, had played on the basketball team and married a distant cousin of mine. He was drafted relatively late in the war, having been deferred for a time to work in the coal mines. Pete Grange's death sticks in my memory as an isolated event, connected to nothing else, and it is only by research in old newspaper files that I have learned he was wounded on 16 June 1945, in a farther field than any of ours, and died three days later.

As we dropped down the hill at the edge of town on our return to the field, Ted gave a sharp whistle and pointed to the bushy slope to the west. A big badger was waddling toward its den, a rare sight so late in the day. There was something comical about its slow but hurried progress, like a little fat man who was late for an appointment. When Len caught sight of it, he grabbed for his pitchfork and brandished it above his head like a javelin, going "huh-huh-huh" with each thrust as though he were striking home.

Len's awakened aggressiveness continued in the field, and he made a feint at me with his pitchfork before he placed the first pile on the corner of the hayrack. When he discovered a field mouse under a pile of hay, he chased it down the furrow and finally speared it on a tine and held it up for us to admire. The sight of the tiny impaled corpse with its naked tail made me shudder, though not from any sympathy for the mouse. I detested the scurrying creatures that suddenly darted out from almost underfoot as you walked through the stubble. Once, before I was born, a mouse had run up the inside of my father's trouser leg while he was working in the hay, and it seemed to me that nothing worse could possibly happen to anyone. Some of our neighbors collected the mice that they killed in a day's haying, threading them on a length of baling wire to make grisly trophies that they displayed to one another as the hayracks passed in the lanes.

Near the end of the load, Len Wight suddenly burst forth with a series of nasal cries. He gestured skyward, and I looked up, thinking it might be a plane flying too high to be heard. It was a golden eagle, down from the cliffs, making lazy circles on its dark wings. Len swung his pitchfork in an ascending arc and went "eh-eh-eh-eh," mimicking the action of an antiaircraft gun. Unaffected, the eagle continued circling, gradually drifting back toward the mountains. The day had begun cloudless, but with the afternoon heat dark thunderheads had gathered over the high plateau. There was little chance that it would rain in the valley, but we sometimes caught the distant rumble of dry thunder, like the fading echo of bombs exploding somewhere far away.

As we approached the barnyard with another load, the fire whistle began to blow. Instinctively we scanned the horizon looking for the plume of smoke. But the siren kept wailing on and on, and after a few moments we could also hear the ringing of the meetinghouse bell. Then cars began to appear on the streets, horns honking. Maggie Young drove right into the yard, leaning on her horn and making the horses shy back against the doubletree.

"The war is over!" she shouted. "The Japs have surrendered. The war is over!"

Grandpa paused only to unharness the team. Then we climbed into the old Dodge and joined the aimless parade, sounding our horn along with the others. After driving up and down the streets of the town, we headed south toward Castle Dale, waving and shouting at the men still working in the fields along the way: "The war is over! The war is over!" When we returned to Poplarhaven, the fire whistle had stopped, but the bell still rang its measured cadence for a long time.

There was no more hauling on that day. The next morning we had to begin by unloading the wagon we had left in the yard. Dad and Uncle Merlin both had a holiday, so it was a family crew on the empty hayrack as we rode out to the farther field. When we reached the crest of the hill at the edge of town, we saw a hayrack stopped at the bottom and a group of men gathered around something on the ground. As we drew abreast, Grandpa slowed the team, and Len Wight, in the middle of the crowd, hoisted the dead badger above his head, curling his lips back from his teeth, grinning proudly as he showed off his prize.

TWENTY-THREE

Goodbye to Poplarhaven

"And the end of all our exploring
Will be to arrive where we started
And know the place for the first time."
　　　　　　　　　—T. S. Eliot, "Little Gidding"

East Mountain, whose rocky escarpment towered above Rowley Flat, just west of town, resembled to my childhood fancy an immense dragon, with a pyramidal peak for a head and a massive, humped body terminating in a tail of foothills. This quiet monster was in no way threatening, however. Whether viewed in the clean light of a summer dawn, or through the mellow haze of an autumnal afternoon, or silhouetted against a darkening sky, it was a secure, familiar presence, a visual anchor in the one horizon that will always seem to me the proper shape of the earth.

Now East Mountain has taken on monstrous associations of another kind as the site of the disastrous Wilberg Mine fire which killed twenty-seven people in December 1984. Actually, they were not the mountain's first victims. I can remember several men who died in the East Mountain coal mines before them, and there were doubtless others that I do not recall. The mines were smaller when I was a boy, mostly family-owned operations with only a handful of employees, and the deaths usually came singly and were mourned in private by family and community.

The multiple-fatality accident that I remember most vividly occurred in the McKinnon mine while I was going to college in Price and living at home. I caught a ride to Poplarhaven with Shelton Wakefield one evening, and as we were crossing the Washboard Flat I proposed that we take in the movie that night at Rosie's place, as we called the drive-in theater that Zen Jensen had built at the edge of town.

Shelton (whose father, Uncle Perry Wakefield, was killed several years later in a mining accident on the slopes of East Mountain) gave me a strange look.

"Haven't you heard? Rosie's dead."

"Rosie?" I said. "What happened?"

"Cave-in. Rosie, and Archie Blackham, and Joe Piccolo."

At the end of our journey we entered a town in mourning. The indoor theater was closed as well as the drive-in. The drugstore was open, but the people there spoke in hushed tones, as if in a mortuary. Like fishermen and soldiers and others who must face danger and possible death in the course of their daily work, miners tend to be superstitious, and in the aftermath of every serious accident there is talk of strange premonitions and omens. It was said that Archie Blackham, the youngest of those killed, had been working his last shift, intending to quit the mine and go back to school. The last shift was always a dangerous time in coalminer lore. Some maintained that you should never make advance plans to quit the mine. If you did, the mine would surely get you. The only safe way was simply not to show up one day. In Archie's case, there was the additional twist that he had no business being in the area of the rockfall. He had finished his work in another part of the mine and without being asked had come to help with the timbering—hurrying (the story ran) as though he were late for an appointment.

Though the accident cast a pall over the community that lasted for some time, it created little stir in the outside world. Even the Salt Lake papers gave it only a few column inches. The Wilberg Mine fire, by contrast, attracted wide attention, which can be ascribed in part to the different scale of the disaster and in part to the temper of the times. The news business has become both more competitive and more "high-tech" in recent years. Satellite transmission allows live televised coverage of events from locations that a few years ago would have been represented only with grainy wirephotos. Along with the greater immediacy made possible by technology has come also a lessened regard for privacy and a willingness to exploit human pain for its audience appeal. The Wilberg disaster, with its days of suspense before it could be determined whether any of the trapped miners had survived, was a natural for television. And it occurred, moreover, during the week before Christmas, which tends to be a slow time in the news business.

Reporters and camera crews poured into the valley, and for several evenings in succession I experienced an unsettling conjunction of the familiar and the strange as the national newscasts opened with a view of the ledges of East Mountain followed by a shot of a reporter standing amid the meager Christmas decorations in the little town park across the street from the mine company offices, which occupy the building where I attended high school. While the places were familiar, the events and most of the names were strange to me, and in that strangeness is an indication of what has happened to the valley in the years since I left it. Only a few of the dead miners had family roots in Emery County. Several others came from the declining coal regions of the eastern United States, from West Virginia, Ohio, Illinois, attracted by what had seemed to be brighter opportunities in the West. The largest group, however, were from Price and other Carbon County towns, mostly descendents of the European immigrants who came in the early years of the century to work in the mines there. When I was a boy, Emery County miners used to commute to Carbon County mines because they preferred to live in their native farm villages. The traffic now runs the other way as scores of Carbon County workers commute to work the Emery County mines.

Poplarhaven as I knew it was a four-generation community. Several of the pioneers lived on into my time. One of my earliest memories is of being taken to see Aunt Mariah Wakefield, who impressed me as tremendously old, a withered-up, bed-ridden woman who seemed to go back to the very creation of the world. I knew many of the second generation, those who had come to Poplarhaven as children or who were born there before the turn of the century. They were the representatives of the community's golden age, the period of greatest vitality, when the meetinghouse was built, and the mill, and the schools, and the brick houses; when the Dramatic Society flourished, presenting sometimes a dozen or more plays in a year, and when Professor Hardee could assemble a chorus that would win the Eisteddfod at Scofield and sing in LDS general conference in Salt Lake City.

My parents belonged to the third generation, born in the first two decades of the twentieth century. They experienced the first major depopulation of the valley as a result of the agricultural depression of the 1920s, which deepened into the Great Depression of the 1930s, exacerbated by severe drought. Yet despite this, they too grew up in vital, active communities with a still-youthful population. In their day, the name Wilberg called up images of pleasure rather than disaster. For the Wilberg family operated a resort, located midway between Poplarhaven and Castle Dale, where young people gathered from all across the valley for the Saturday night dances.

My generation was the fourth, and the last Poplarhaven generation. Born during the Depression, we grew up in the 1940s and 1950s in a community still rich with life but slowly dying, like the rows of Lombardy poplars that remained straight and tall but with rotting heartwood and gaps where fallen trees had once stood. I started school with forty-seven classmates, a number which grew to about seventy when we reached high school and were joined by the kids from Cleveland and Elmo then dwindled again to some forty-odd by graduation. Each succeeding class was smaller, with fewer and fewer young people staying in the valley to begin new families. Between 1955 and 1965, the population of the community fell by almost half, and among those who remained the median age was over fifty. The high school was closed, the old meetinghouse demolished, and the Prickly Pear Flat was littered with empty houses, sagging barns, junked cars, and dead trees.

In the late 1960s and early 1970s, two developments occurred which arrested this steady decline. The first was a revulsion against urban life that sent numerous people fleeing from the cities back to rural areas. Some of them found their way to our valley—not enough to reverse the trend of depopulation, but for the first time in many years people were moving into the region. Unlike the original settlers, who wanted to live together in villages, most of the new people were trying to get away from close neighbors. They preferred to live on farms, which they called ranches, and as a result land values soared. Some of the natives sold their farms for more money than they had earned from them in a lifetime of hard work.

The second development, and the one that worked the most profound and lasting transformation of the community, was the energy industry. Attracted by the large reserves of high-grade bituminous coal, Utah Power and Light Company built two large generating plants in the valley and developed mines and haulage systems to supply them with fuel. The power plants increased the county's tax base dramatically, and construction and mining jobs brought an influx of new residents. For a few years, Emery County boasted the highest per capita income in the state. Much of that money went to highly skilled construction workers who never really belonged to the community but simply camped out in trailers while the job lasted and took their paychecks home to the Wasatch Front cities. But new jobs were also created for local residents, and it seemed for a time that the long-held dream that the valley's young people could remain at home would be realized. To some extent it was realized. There are once again young families in the valley, and homes and schools and commercial buildings have sprung up in towns that had seen little new construction in the previous half century. But with the benefits of industrialization have come its problems. Jobs in the power plants and coal mines pay well for those who have them but are subject to the ups and downs that plague the energy industry. Even before the Wilberg Mine disaster, cutbacks in construction plans and reduced demand for coal had resulted in widespread layoffs in a region where other employment possibilities are almost nonexistent.

So life goes on in the town on the Prickly Pear Flat, and in the other towns which nestle in the shadow of the high plateau and which now have two or three times as many residents as they had when I was a boy. But they are different communities from the ones that I knew. Our way of life was in many respects closer to that of the 1890s than to that of the 1980s. Poplarhaven is no more. It has disappeared along with the brick houses, and the barns, and the meetinghouse, and the Town Ditch, and the old grade school with its varnished floorboards. Only a few signs remain that it ever existed: an isolated Lombardy poplar here, a half-dead orchard there; the mill, and the public corral, and a certain vista across the fields; and, hopefully, these few essays which represent my own tribute to a place and its people, a personal goodbye to Poplarhaven.